CHANGING THE GAME

CHANGING THE GAME

HOW TO PROFIT FROM
YOUR PASSION FOR SPORTS

By a Wall Street Investment Manager
WILLIAM HALL, III

ISBN: 098494271X
ISBN-13: 978-0-9849427-1-8

This edition published by Bookworm Sports.
For more information, visit www.bookwormsports.com.

Table of Contents

Introduction: Wagering the Wall Street Way   ix

Wall Street and the Sports Line   x
The Sports Wagering Paradox   xii
The Games We Play   xv
Back to the Paradox   xvii
The Businesslike Bettor   xvii
Sports Betting — A *Winnable* Game   xviii

Chapter One: Why Bet?   1

To Get to the Next Level, Sell the Beans or Place a Bet   2
Show Me the Money   3
Don't Be Average   5
Gambling? I Don't Think So!   5
The Scorecard — A Compound Money Machine   7
The Scorecard Tells the Story   8
The Power of Thinking Like Bill Belichick   10
The Math Works Big-Time   11
Mark Teixeira and Warren Buffett Make the
    Big Money; So Can You   13
A Sports Book: The New York Stock Exchange of
    Sports Wagering   14

Chapter Two: The Sports Betting Game   15

The Point Spread   15
Sports Books: The Games Are Played Here   16
The Commission: A Success Fee   18
Balancing the Books   19
Leonard the Line Maker   20
Amateur Andy   21
Streaking Steve   21
Louie the Loser   22
Last Chance Vance   23
Frank the Fan   23
The Intelligent Bettor   24

Chapter Three: Getting Started — The Fundamentals   25

The Line Maker Is Not Your Enemy   26
The Contrarian Versus the Competition   27
The Five Essentials for Successful Sports Betting   27
A Better Model: *Get In and Win*   28
Superior Information: See the Invisible Gorilla   30
Controlling Risk: Don't Swing at Every Pitch   34
Careful Money Management: Crank Out the Singles   36
Discipline in Staying the Course Will Get You to Your Goal   37
Successful Sports Betting: A Review of the Essentials   38

Chapter Four: Searching for Value   41

Value in Investing   43
Billy Beane and Value   45
Diogenes, Billy Beane and the Intelligent Bettor   47
The Gold Is in the Numbers   47
Break Through the Box Score   48
Probability x Payoff = Team Value   52
You Pay a High Price for a Cheery Consensus   55
It's All About Value   57
Margin of Safety   58

Chapter Five: A Playbook for Finding Value   61

Value Ratings: The Perfect Predictor   63
Value Ratings Applied, Using the NFL as an Example   67
Updating NFL Value Ratings   70
Applying and Updating NBA Value Ratings   72
With the Value Rating, You Are 80 Percent of the Way There   76
Wall Street Uses DuPont Analysis   77
Score Sheets Put You in the Winning Seat   78
Fantasy Fanatics Love the NFL Score Sheets   79
The NBA Score Sheet   84
Check the Alignment   87
Alignment and Margin of Safety — A Powerful Combination   88
A Replay of the Playbook for Finding Value   90

Chapter Six: The Money Management Game Plan 93

Keep It Simple and Be Selective 94
How Much to Bet: The Five Percent Rule 94
Not Too High and Not Too Low, but Just Right 95
Money Mistakes 96
Get Up Enough Shots 97
Streaks 101
It Hurts to Lose, and Here Is the Proof 104
Why Zebras Don't Get Ulcers and Sports Bettors Do 105
There Is Hope: Losing Is Part of Winning 106
In Case of Emergency, Do This 106
Imitating Ulysses 107

Chapter Seven: Reading the Line and Shopping for Value 109

How to Read the Board 109
Why Lines Move: Not All Point Spreads Are Equal 112
Off-Standard Point Spreads 114
The Battle of the Books: The Internet vs. Las Vegas 116
Attention Value Shoppers! 118
Timing Can Add Value 119

Chapter Eight: Choose Your Path for Financial Reward   121

    Investor or Business Owner?   121
    Investors Look at the Scorecard   123
    When It Seems Too Good to Be True, It Really Is   129
    Your Own Sports Franchise   134
    A Plan for Business Success   134
    Cash in Hand Every Three Months   135
    The Sports Wagering Cash Flow Plan   136

Chapter Nine: Hidden Treasures   159

    Proposition Bets: Win or Lose, a Win-Win Situation   159
    Betting on Totals: A Simple Path to Success   162
    Money Lines: It's Not As Hard as You Think   163
    A Little Money Line Math   164
    Money Line Value   169
    Baseball Uses the Money Line   170
    The Basics of Baseball Betting: Is It
       Hitting or Pitching?   171
    Pay Attention to Starting Pitching   171
    Baseball's Dime Line — A Bettor's Bargain   173
    Why Is Baseball So Good for Sports Bettors?   174
    Betting on Props, Totals and Money Lines
       Means More Opportunities   175

Chapter Ten: Buyer Beware — The Seven Deadly Bets   177

    Parlays   177
    Teasers   183
    Sweethearts   184
    Football Cards   185
    Baseball's Run Lines   187
    The Futures Are Not Good   189
    TV: There's a Reason They Call It the Idiot Box   190
    Don't Be a Pig   191

    Glossary of Get In and Win
       Sports Wagering Terms   193

Introduction:
Wagering the Wall Street Way

*The fact is, we have all been a good deal puzzled
because the affair is so simple, and yet baffles us
all together. It was hidden in plain sight, so no
one could discover it.*

Edgar Allan Poe
"The Purloined Letter"

For a long time in the United States, we have truly been "a good deal
puzzled" about what it means to place a wager on a sporting event. Sports
betting conjures images of cigar-chomping toughs in Las Vegas, or desper-
ate losers huddled around video terminals in grimy gambling parlors. We
read about football gamblers who are so obsessed they spend every waking
hour glued to multiple TV screens, screaming bets over the phone to bookies, blowing entire paychecks and destroying their families, much like an
alcoholic. Indeed, Gamblers Anonymous provides support for those whose
addiction to betting transcends all other considerations.

But while our society generally regards alcohol as a pleasant social diversion that only some are incapable of enjoying responsibly, sports betting is
viewed almost universally as a dangerous vice that must be discouraged
and even banned. And in reality, many of the same state governments that
prohibit sports betting are the biggest hypocrites, shamelessly promoting

gambling on their own lotteries, which unlike informed sports wagers are genuinely exploitive games of chance. In fact, over the past 70 years, the number of states with legal games of pure chance — from lotteries to slot machines — has jumped from one to 48. [1]

And yet, as an experienced Wall Street analyst and sports fanatic, I can tell you that placing a thoughtful wager on a sporting event is not gambling at all. Sports wagering, when pursued sensibly, involves the same deductive reasoning skills as trading a put or a call option in the financial markets. There is no difference between the two activities except how and where the transaction takes place. At their core, they both involve making a calculated assessment of the likely outcome of a certain future event and an exchange of money. [2]

Wall Street and the Sports Line

Wall Street is a frenetic place. If it were a football game, each team would be running the no-huddle offense — that is, receivers and running backs would be constantly in motion; the defense would be blitzing again and again; and the quarterback would be running up to the line of scrimmage after each completion, calling plays through cupped hands while directing his receivers where to line up. The game of Wall Street is a non-stop search for clarity. It takes place on the stage of a constantly changing world, and it pits some of the best and brightest minds around the globe against each other in pursuit of profits — relentlessly searching and sifting for that one bit of information, that one piece of the puzzle that gives them an edge over all the others in the marketplace.

For an avid sports fan such as myself, watching college and professional games — and following my favorite teams in the sports pages — provides

---

1 Davies, Richard O. and Abram, Richard G., *Betting the Line, Sports Wagering in American Life*; 2001, The Ohio State University Press.

2 While sports betting and options trading have many similarities, they are both distinctly different from investing in long-duration assets that produce gains over time. Purchasing a stock, bond or mutual fund for future capital appreciation is an investment activity. Conversely, options traders and sports bettors earn speculative short-term profits.

an entertaining diversion from the world of global finance. It serves as a distraction, a chance to recall great memories associated with sports and the people I shared them with. Who could forget Joe Namath's bold prediction that his Jets would beat the heavily favored Colts in Super Bowl III, and then watching Namath actually lead them to victory on the field? I will always remember the first time that I walked onto the field, as a 7-year-old ball boy, at the historic Cotton Bowl before a University of Texas football game; all I could say was "Wow!" Or how I excited I was when my dad took me to the legendary War Memorial Coliseum on Kentucky's campus to watch the Wildcats take on Tennessee in one of the SEC's fiercest basketball rivalries. Even as an adult, I experience that familiar adrenaline rush every time I enter Fenway Park (where the grass seems so green and the grilled hot dogs smell so good); it feels like I'm on hallowed ground. For me, and maybe for you, sports has significantly influenced my perspective on life.

But like most of us who are not professional athletes, I compartmentalized my love of sports and my work as a financial advisor; Bill the sports fan and Bill the investment manager coexisted in my mind, but they occupied completely separate spaces. That all changed one day several years ago. While flipping through the newspapers, I ran across a stock option price quote similar to the following in the financial section:

```
Call Option IBM
Expiration: Jan 2002
Strike Price: $80; Cost $4
```

Then in the sports section, I noticed:

```
New England Patriots        -7.5        -350
Minnesota Vikings           u46         +280
```

Right there, it hit me. These two seemingly different and disparate pieces of information were actually the exact same thing.

How could this be? One listing concerned the stock market and the other presented the odds for a football game. The stock market and sports betting — how much further apart could two things be? But for a sports fanatic trained in mathematical models and sophisticated market trading programs, the two worlds had finally intersected. Because when you really think about it, both are what finance gurus call *options*. The IBM option gives you the right to buy the underlying stock of IBM at a predetermined price; in our example, that right expired in January of 2002. And the odds quoted on the football game represent the price you would have to pay to place a bet, depending on who you think will win the game.

Both are contractual financial arrangements that require the assessment of the likely outcome of a future event. Mathematicians, financial analysts and other numbers geeks call this probability theory. For the IBM call option, you are being asked to make a judgment about the short-term movement of the stock price during a specific period of time. For the Patriots-Vikings game, you are being asked to predict the likely winner — and your "option" expires when the game clock winds down to zero.

By the way, an investor who bought that particular IBM stock option would have made a profit of $11 per contract when the position closed on January 15, 2002, and IBM shares were priced at $91. And in the football game, the Patriots won 24-17 but did not cover the spread, leaving those who bet on the victors empty-handed. The key here is that the "spreads" for both the call option and the football game were determined by real money changing hands between people with different points of view, because for each buyer there was a seller on the other side.

The Sports Wagering Paradox

Since they are really the same thing, why should investment management be such a privileged profession while sports betting is viewed with such disdain? I find the paradox to be quite perplexing. Because both activities involve the analysis of financial options, why has no one made a compelling case comparing the two? Why, in the U.S., where hedge fund managers and day traders treat the investment markets like their own personal casinos as they make hundreds of speculative transactions (many over the Internet), is sports wagering synonymous with gambling?[3] Why, in Great Britain, is it a normal part of daily life to bet on any American or international sporting event? In fact, you can walk in off the street and place a legal wager on the Celtics vs. Lakers game in the most exclusive part of the financial district in London, just as easily as you can in the smallest town in the European countryside. But in most places in the U.S., sports wagering is illegal except under certain special circumstances. How can the NFL and the NBA think about going global when both leagues publicly oppose sports betting?

These are interesting questions to ponder because on Wall Street I have learned that when there is inconsistency in the global markets, there is usually money to be made by resolving it. And recently, there have been some significant developments that demonstrate others are thinking the same way. In fact, *The Wall Street Journal* has begun publishing a sports section that includes the projected score and the wagering line for professional and college sports games.

And despite their public stance against sports betting, professional sports leagues and the National Collegiate Athletic Association have been entering into bold new marketing relationships with gambling interests, preparing themselves for the day when sports betting will be legalized. The National Basketball Association has been the most open about the inevitable legalization of sports betting. "We have a global business where many countries like the U.K. and China have legalized sports betting," NBA Deputy Commissioner Adam Silver told *USA Today* last year. "We can't live with our heads in the sand and pound our fists that we don't want

---

3   If you have any doubt about the speculative nature of hedge funds, read Roger Lowenstein's captivating book *When Genius Failed*. It is a true account of the rise and fall of the world's largest hedge fund, Long-Term Capital Management, and how its partners thought the fund's finely tuned computer models had tamed the genie of risk and would allow them to bet on the future (with near mathematical certainty, using enormous leverage) to create limitless wealth. At the heart of the fund was a group of brainy, Ph.D.-certified arbitrageurs. In fact, two had won the Nobel Prize. At its peak, the fund had entered into thousands of derivative contracts, which had intertwined it with every financial institution on Wall Street. These contracts, essentially side bets on market prices, represented a mind-boggling $1 trillion worth of market exposure.

betting on our games. We realize there is enormous interest in betting on our games. Over time, there is no question that it will be more accepted."

Even more recently, in May of 2010, National Football League owners voted to allow teams to sign deals with state-sponsored lotteries for the first time. They are following the path blazed by Major League Baseball clubs like the New York Yankees, the New York Mets and the Boston Red Sox.

Meanwhile, if college athletic leaders are opposed to gambling, you would be hard-pressed to tell from their venue choices. The West Coast Conference holds its postseason basketball tournament at the Orleans Hotel's arena in Las Vegas, and the Western Athletic Conference will do the same in 2011 and 2012. And former Indiana basketball coach–turned–ESPN analyst Bobby Knight and former CBS analyst Billy Packer co-hosted a TV show for Fox Sports Network, *Survive and Advance* — analyzing the 2009 NCAA men's basketball tournament — that was broadcast from the Wynn resort in the heart of the Las Vegas strip.

More to the point, in 2009 the prestigious bond trading firm Cantor Fitzgerald took over management of the sports book at M Resort, a new Las Vegas casino. The Wall Street company, which transformed the resort's sports parlor into a businesslike space filled with cubicles and computer screens much like a trading floor, also views sports betting as a form of derivatives trading.

But while sports wagering is much like options and derivatives trading, there is one significant difference. In the U.S., sports betting is against the law everywhere except Nevada.[4] Of course, that hasn't stopped underground sports bookmaking activities in every state. (When authorities do crack down on sports betting they generally prosecute the bookies, not the individual bettors.)

An even bigger betting market has sprung up on the Internet. It is common knowledge that you can access a number of licensed and reputable foreign sports books, some operating in England, Canada and Australia, over the Internet. And the websites of ESPN, *Sporting News*, *USA Today* and Fox Sports show not only the betting lines for all the professional and

---

4 Oregon has a lottery that allows betting on professional football games. Canada has no national prohibition against placing a sports bet, and allows Internet sports betting.

college games, but also a detailed comparison among various Internet sports books so you can get the best deal.

The Nevada Gaming Commission says that sports bettors wagered $2.5 billion in the state's 181 licensed sports books in 2009 (91 percent of all bets were on football, basketball and baseball games). Yet according to *USA Today* sports analyst Danny Sheridan, Nevada's take is "a drop in the bucket," with far more betting action today being conducted through Internet sports books both legal and illegal, offshore sports books, fantasy sports leagues, "March Madness" pools and local bookies. Sheridan puts the total annual figure for sports betting at close to $300 billion — about the same as the gross domestic product of Switzerland.

Regardless, it is illegal to make a sports bet from your computer if you are located anywhere in the United States — including Nevada. As a respected financial advisor, I personally do not make illegal wagers and am not advising you to do so. I will, however, tell you that any money you earn from sports betting — legally or otherwise — must be reported as income to the IRS. (Report it as "other income" on line 21 of your federal tax return, Form 1040).

So if you are a U.S. citizen and plan to wager legally using the information in this book, you will need to go to a location where sports wagering is allowed — such as Las Vegas, England, Canada, Mexico or many Caribbean nations. Should you go to England, Canada[5], Mexico or the Caribbean, take your computer with you because you can choose to place your wagers at a local sports betting parlor or over the Internet, where you have hundreds of options at your fingertips. If you go to Nevada, leave your computer at home because only betting in licensed establishments is legal there.

The Games We Play

Sports are about having fun, of course. But fun doesn't fully explain the fascination of sports; there is something else going on. Sports are one

---

5 In-casino sports betting in Canada is allowed but is limited to parlay wagers.

of the few entertainment options where the outcome is truly unknown. Think about movies for a moment. When you went to see the Harry Potter movies, did you ever actually think Harry would lose, and that the Dark Lord would ultimately prevail over the Order of the Phoenix?[6] But a sporting event is a real-life drama being played out right before our eyes. And sometimes the outcome is wildly different than anyone expects. Consider the 2004 American League Championship Series between the New York Yankees and the Boston Red Sox. Even though the Yankees and Red Sox had split their regular-season matchups, the Yankees started out hot and won the first three games of championship play. In the best-of-seven series, that meant the Yankees needed only one more win to advance to the World Series, while the downtrodden Red Sox faced the daunting task of winning four games in a row. Any reasonable person would have expected the Yankees to play in the World Series, sending the Red Sox back to Boston to contemplate "the curse of the Babe" and what might have been, yet one more time.

But that's not what happened. The Red Sox won game four, and then five, six and seven, and baseball history was made. (The Sox went on to win the World Series for the first time since 1918.) The fact that we don't know the final outcome is what attracts us to sporting events. We love the drama, the stories about the players and the intellectual challenge of trying to predict the ending.

Lots of sports fans are content to enjoy that intellectual challenge for its own rewards — the thrill of watching their favorite team win, and the vicarious pleasure of cheering on players who are making millions of dollars doing what they love. But for other sports fans, the challenge of predicting the outcome of a game is even more exciting when, like the players, they too stand a chance to profit from the result.[7] Their betting activity comes in many forms: the $5 office pool on the NCAA basketball tournament or the World Series; the weekly meeting of the fantasy football league; putting

---

6 It is interesting to note that some of the most watched television shows, like award shows and reality shows, are similar to sports in that the ending is not known.

7 Players don't, or at least should not, bet on their own games; to use the Wall Street analogy, that would be considered insider trading, which is illegal. But they certainly profit by winning games and championships!

down 10 bucks on a six-team parlay card with a bartender at the neighborhood tavern; or even making a $20 bet on the Super Bowl. And for serious bettors, it involves picking winners against the point spread or the money line. Anyway you look at it, wagering has become an important part of the enormous popularity of sports.

Back to the Paradox

Most sports betting is small, recreational and largely uninformed — based on impulse and inspired by team loyalty. It's exactly the kind of betting that you *shouldn't* do if you plan on taking it seriously. Yet that careless, crapshoot version of gambling around the office water cooler is the one version of sports betting that is largely condoned in America; authorities don't mount gambling sting operations on office betting pools.

On the other hand, organized, sensible sports betting is an intellectual exercise in which research, unemotional analysis of data and a disciplined approach to allocating capital are crucial to success. Like any form of entrepreneurship, a prudent system of money management and a long-range strategy are required. It embodies the essential values of the American free enterprise system — rewarding hard work, intelligence, research and judgment. So why is it that when these traits are applied to a businessman or a successful investor they are viewed positively, but when applied to someone wagering on sports there is condemnation? It would seem that a profound moral confusion exists in the United States as it relates to wagering on sporting events.

The Businesslike Bettor

The sports wagering market is not perceived as a true financial market — and that simple fact is what makes it easier to make money in sports wagering than in the "real" markets. In sport wagering, the informed player who conducts himself in a businesslike manner has an advantage over the other players in a way that cannot be duplicated in the financial markets. While it may not seem like it (and I'll explain why later), you are really competing against the other bettors — not the sports book — when wagering on sports. And it is precisely for that reason that your *biggest single ally in sports wagering is the overall mediocrity and uninformed actions of the casual sports bettor.*

Sports Betting — A *Winnable* Game

To understand why wagering on sports represents a real moneymaking opportunity, compare it again to trading in the financial markets. Large institutions and full-time professionals dominate the financial markets. These professionals have more information and have done more extensive research than the general investing public. They understand the companies whose financial instruments they trade and the markets in which the transactions are executed. The success of their organizations and their own compensation is completely dependent on their trading activities. In the financial markets, it is very hard for individual investors to consistently outperform the professionals over any extended period of time.

By contrast, the vast majority of sports wagers are placed by individuals who view betting as entertainment — not a business. They do it because it is fun to bet on the home team, or because they got a hot tip from a friend. If they win, it is "found" money. If they lose, they still have enjoyed having some "action" on the game. So for the serious sports bettor, the competition is slim.

Think of it this way. There is a lot of very current and accurate information available about every professional football team. Information on each game, each player and all types of cumulative statistics can be easily obtained from the Internet and other sources. In addition to all these facts, there is also a wealth of qualitative analysis that can be derived from sources such as local newspaper columns, coaches' shows and media guides. If you are passionate about sports, you are probably familiar with this information and how much of it there is. Also, you probably have a feel for how the information can be used to gain insight into the team and its performance in a specific game or over an entire season. Well, it might surprise you to learn that most casual sports bettors don't pay much attention to all that free information or don't know how to apply it properly. They simply bet their gut. Therefore, it is possible for those who are serious about sports and familiar with the analytical tools to have an information advantage over much of the sports betting public.

Compare this with your ability to analyze a publicly traded company. As in sports, all investors in public companies have access to the same information and disclosures required by the Securities and Exchange Commission. But those public disclosures provide only a fraction of the information needed to truly understand a company, its prospects and all the intricacies of its traded securities. Major institutions and research organizations spend millions of dollars analyzing public companies so that they can trade for their own benefit in the financial markets. In the financial markets, it just isn't likely that you will be able to gain an information advantage over Goldman Sachs, J.P. Morgan, Merrill Lynch or Fidelity.

Imagine if Wall Street portfolio managers ignored company earnings reports and analysts' recommendations, then simply bought stocks based on some gut feeling. Not many people would put their retirement nest egg into the Vanguard Gut Feeling Fund. Yet that is how billions of dollars are wagered on sports.

Betting on sports and winning consistently does not require a stratospheric IQ, abnormally keen insights, an Ivy League education or inside information. What is needed is a sound analytical framework so that you can approach sports wagering in a businesslike manner and prevent emotion from creeping into the process. That is why I created the *Get In and Win* System. It incorporates time-tested business principles and valuation techniques used by the most successful Wall Street traders. The *Get In and Win* System contains all the information you need to make money betting on sports.[8]

By following the easy-to-understand and easily applied *Get In and Win* System, you can achieve highly profitable results. How much money you ultimately make will depend on the effort and intellect you apply to the

---

8 The *Get In and Win* methods are based on stochastic game theory, and the reliability of the system has been rigorously tested and verified using sophisticated statistical techniques: multi-variable regression analysis and Monte Carlo simulations.

wagering process. Moreover, the sillier the behavior of the other bettors, the greater the opportunity for you, the businesslike bettor.

As you progress through *Get In and Win*, you will learn real-world tactics to succeed from a hypothetical master called the Intelligent Bettor. You will also learn game plans to avoid, from Amateur Andy, Louie the Loser, Frank the Fan, Streaking Steve and Last Chance Vance. You will be taught how to place winning bets by compiling *Scorecards*, *Value Ratings, Score Sheets* and *Poisson Props* — all of which are original strategies (based on proven investment practices) that reveal the winning sports information that's hidden in plain sight. You'll learn the importance of a *Margin of Safety* and *Win Rates*, how to recognize *Hidden Treasures*, and how to construct a *Money Management Game Plan*. And Sammy Swish and Arnold Airball will teach you about the psychology associated with winning and losing streaks. When you are done, you will be fully prepared to get in the game and make big profits over the long term.

Possessing a sound process for obtaining useful information, knowing which tools to use for each job, and having the necessary discipline, knowledge and judgment are all attributes that you need to be a successful investor on Wall Street. Sports wagering is no different. Use the *Get In and Win* System to wager the Wall Street way, and the odds will be with you.

Why Bet?

"The difficulty lies, not in the new ideas, but in escaping from the old ones."

Economist John Maynard Keynes

This book will give you an inside track on creating wealth in a way that you probably never thought possible. Did you ever imagine that you would be able to make big money by watching and following your favorite sports and teams? Well, you can. All it takes is having the *right* information, interpreting that information correctly and being businesslike in your approach. In doing so, you will use the triumphs and victories of the best coaches, players and teams to help you achieve personal success, sports-guru status and wealth. That is why I developed the *Get In and Win* System, so you can get in on the fun too and make some money at the same time.

Betting on sports is exciting and fast paced, requiring mastery of many situational strategies. To be successful, preparation and precision are essential. That's why it's imperative to have a well thought-out game plan so you can execute flawlessly and score when the pressure is on. It is the precise execution of a proper process that produces winning results. *Get In and Win* has all the right plays so you can wager with confidence when the game is on the line. When applied consistently over the long term, the *Get In and Win* approach provides the strategic advantage required to earn real profits in the sports betting market.

To Get to the Next Level, Sell the Beans or Place a Bet

Jim Rogers, the highly regarded investor who founded the Quantum Fund[9] with George Soros, knows exactly what it takes to be successful in the financial markets. In his book _Hot Commodities_, Rogers explains how trading commodities helped sharpen his financial expertise: "I suddenly realized that by studying a commodity or two I began to see the world anew. Suddenly, I was no longer just eating breakfast but thinking about how the weather in Brazil might cause coffee and sugar prices to go up or down, how Kellogg's stock price would respond to higher corn prices, and whether the demand for bacon (cut from pork bellies) would decline down during the summer months. Knowing about the commodities markets does much more than make your breakfast more interesting, it makes you a better investor."

Rogers goes on to explain: "Once you understand, for example, why the prices of copper, lead and other metals have been rising, it is only a baby step toward understanding why the economies in countries such as Canada, Australia, Chile and Peru, all rich in metal resources, are doing well; why shares in companies with investments in metal producing countries are worth checking out; why some real estate prices are likely to rise; and how you might even be able to make some money investing in hotel or super-market chains in countries where consumers suddenly have more money than usual."

Rogers caps it off by saying, "If you really want to learn about finance, sell the beans!"

And it's the same with sports wagering. Once you place a bet on a game, your entire sports experience changes for the better, because you now have a vested financial interest in the outcome. No longer are you the casual observer sitting in the bleachers just thinking about how your favorite players are doing. When you have some money at risk, a wonderful change occurs and you start seeing the game through the eyes of the players,

---

9. Established in 1973, the Quantum Fund returned 4,200% over the next 10 years while the S&P 500 returned 47% over the same period.

coaches and general managers. Wagering on a sporting event sharpens your focus and deepens your understanding of the game matchups in an exciting way. Placing a wager transforms your perspective from observer to participant, taking your enjoyment and knowledge of sports to the next level. To get fully engaged in the sports you love, place a thoughtful wager and start to profit from your passion for sports.

Show Me the Money

Sports are about competition and entertainment, of course, but anyone who follows professional and college sports knows that they are also big business. Team owners like Jerry Jones of the Dallas Cowboys and the late George Steinbrenner of the New York Yankees amassed fortunes by marketing and promoting their franchises. General managers and athletic directors are compensated like royalty to choose the players and coaches who will represent their teams. Those coaches make millions of dollars annually, and the players (the professional ones) are paid even more money to shoot a basketball, complete a pass, and swing a bat, as well as endorse products. The money train doesn't end with the teams. Media outlets (which rake in ad dollars and cable subscription fees) employ armies of sports reporters and commentators, some of whom are as famous as the players, to say nothing of all the support staff. Licensing deals fill the coffers of clothing and souvenir manufacturers and retailers, who in turn create jobs for thousands of people. And the local businesses that surround the sports venues rely on the popularity of their hometown teams for financial success.

Where does all of that money ultimately come from? The answer is simple. It comes from you, the fan — and the more the athletes make, the more you pay. I remember when I was a young man thinking it was outrageous when the best tickets to a Red Sox game topped 10 bucks. If I didn't want to buy the tickets, I could always choose to watch the games for free on TV. Today, those choices seem like a bargain when the best infield box seats at Fenway Park cost more than $300 each — if you can even get them. In fact, Red Sox tickets have become so hard to come by that most fans are lucky if they can get their hands on tickets to a single game each year. The rest of the time, they pay their cable company about $45 a month to watch the excitement on TV.

But you don't have to sit on the sidelines and pay. You can get in the game too and make your passion for sports pay *you*. In fact, you can earn enough money betting on sports to buy season tickets to every one of your favorite teams, and still come out way ahead. With the right system and a little discipline, you'll soon have Jerry Jones, Bill Parcells and Peyton Manning putting money in your bank account each week during football season. Basketball presents even more profit-making opportunities, since the teams play even more frequently. And baseball makes it possible to really get your cash flow rolling, with each team playing 162 games during a season that stretches out over seven months.

To make money from sports, all you have to do is learn to make intelligent sports bets. Wagering on sports provides an exciting financial opportunity for both the serious player who is looking to make significant profits from his wagers and the recreational bettor who just wants to generate some spare cash from his hobby. Think about it. Nobody goes to the movies, the ballet, a rock concert or a museum and walks out with more money than when he walked in. How many people can generate a significant source of cash flow doing something they really enjoy with a relatively small investment?

Wagering on sports provides terrific opportunities. But sports wagering must be approached as if you are investing in the financial markets or running a business. To be successful, you must be informed and disciplined, and apply sound financial principles. And above all, you must have a system that provides you with an edge over your competition, the other sports bettors.

My *Get In and Win* System provides a complete game plan that gives you the moneymaking strategies required to successfully compete in the sports wagering markets. The *Get In and Win* System will help you sift through the reams of sports information available and focus only on the statistics that will be most profitable to you. It's inspired by many of the principles found in Michael Lewis' best-selling book *Moneyball*, which details how the Oakland Athletics beat conventional wisdom and fielded a winning baseball team without spending a lot of money; Ben Graham's iconic investment treatise, *The Intelligent Investor*; and, my own experiences working on Wall Street.

Don't Be Average

Swear to yourself not to be an average person, at least as it relates to your sports betting activities. Like many forms of investing, sports wagering is a zero-sum game — meaning that for every dollar committed, someone will win the money and someone else will lose it. During the course of a season, the average sports bettor will lose more than he wins because of incomplete information, bad strategy and poor money management — but you don't have to be average.

In all other fields of life, it is taken for granted that some people do things better than others. Kobe Bryant shoots a basketball better than most. Bill Belichick is recognized as a great football coach. Warren Buffett is widely regarded as one of the world's best investors. And Vladimir Ashkenazy is renowned worldwide as a master pianist. Why would anyone think that sports wagering is any different? If you do it well, there is money to be made wagering on sports. Don't let the naysayers convince you otherwise.

The *Get In and Win* System will show you how to bet smart. By doing so, you won't win all the time — no one does — but *you will win more often than you lose*, possibly far more often. And because you will be spreading your bets over many different games every week, you will come out ahead.

Gambling? I Don't Think So!

There are a number of misconceptions about sports wagering, so let's get the big one out of the way first. Sports wagering is not gambling. When it is done in a serious and professional way, sports wagering involves skill and a reasoned assessment of the odds. By contrast, *gambling is nothing but luck*. Gambling lacks any knowledge of cause and effect and is simply a game of random chance. When gambling, the player places himself before the unknown and seeks only the grace of the deity known as Fortune.

Games such as roulette, slot machines, lotteries and dice are examples of gambling where skill is completely eliminated and the results are random.[10] Gambling is simply hoping that a random chance or event will bring a favorable outcome.

Gambling plays no more a part in informed sports wagering than it does in deciding how much to pay for a financial instrument known as a *call option*. A call option allows the owner to control a specific number of shares of stock, without actually owning them, for a fixed period (usually three to six months). Using call options, investors can leverage their capital and earn high returns in a short period of time. Yes, one could leave it completely to chance when deciding how much to pay for a call option, but experienced market professionals always make an informed assessment as to the price being asked, and the likelihood of the desired outcome, before exchanging their money for the option. In the same way, sensible sports bettors evaluate the odds before placing a wager. An understanding of probability theory and a reasoned judgment as to likely outcomes are essential for success in both activities.

We commonly hear people say, "I *speculated* on that stock" or "I *traded* that stock." But how many times do you hear "I *wagered* on that stock" or "I *bet* on that stock?" They all mean the same thing, which is simply "I exchanged money for the right to own the stock with the expectation of a short-term profit." We could just as easily say, "I *speculated* on the Patriots-Eagles game" or "I *traded* the Patriots-Eagles game." So don't let the commonly held misperceptions about sports wagering, many of them related to terminology, stand in your way.

---

10 Blackjack and poker are other casino games where the application of mathematics, specifically probability theory, can provide the thoughtful player with a skill-based advantage. In his best-selling book, *The Quants*, Scott Patterson (a writer for *The Wall Street Journal*) tells the true story of how a brilliant new breed of mathematicians were inspired by the card-counting strategies introduced by Ed Thorpe, Ph.D., in his popular book *Beat the Dealer: A Winning Strategy for the Game of Twenty-One*, to develop a number of complex market trading strategies that have emerged to dominate much of the financial system.

The Scorecard — A Compound Money Machine

Winning money wagering on sports is not difficult, but it does require a commitment. Winning takes information, judgment, discipline and time. Why time? Why, you might ask, can't you just jump right in, hoping to start raking in the big bucks this afternoon? Actually, you can. The trouble is, you will also lose many of your bets; it's a fact you have to accept. Nobody's perfect and losing is part of winning. But with my system, *you will win more often than you lose.* So it is over time, not overnight, that you will really see the compounded benefits of your wins. Legend has it that Albert Einstein once said compounded savings was the greatest invention in human history. Regardless of whether Einstein actually made that observation, investment compounding (making money on money) is indeed powerful; it has made investment icon Warren Buffett one of the wealthiest people in the world.[11]

---

11 Charlie Munger, Warren Buffett's longtime investment partner, has said on numerous occasions, "Understanding both the power of compound interest and the difficulty of getting it is the heart and soul of understanding a lot of things."

Well, the compounding available to the successful sports bettor is far superior to the compounding you can reap as a stock market investor. To prove it, let's take a look at what I call the Scorecard, which is really a compounding table for sports wagering.

The Scorecard Tells the Story

Scorecard 1.1 shows that the potential returns for the informed sports bettor are indeed incredible. Starting with just $1,000 of cash, Scorecard 1.1 presents the annual net winnings that will result from making 20 equal wagers of $50 per week at certain winning percentages (Win Rates), assuming a 50-week year. Scorecard 1.1 tells us that if you consistently have a Win Rate of 60 percent, you can earn $8,000 on $1,000 of beginning capital. At the end of the year, you would have $9,000 — the $1,000 that you started with plus $8,000 of winnings. On Wall Street, we refer to that as an "8X" return, because you are getting back eight times your beginning invested capital at the end of one year! In 25 years of professional money management, I have seen some, but not many, investment opportunities that offer that kind of moneymaking potential.

Scorecard 1.1

- **$1,000 beginning capital**

- **20 wagers per week ($50 per game)**

Win Rate	Net Annual Winnings
60%	$ 8,000
65%	$13,250
70%	$18,500
75%	$23,750
80%	$29,000
85%	$34,250

Before going forward, let's define some terms. In this book, I will use the term *Win Rate* to refer to the percentage of successful wagers that you make. For example, if you place 10 bets and win six of them, your Win Rate will be 60 percent. Likewise, if you place 20 bets and win 12 of them, you will also have a Win Rate of 60 percent. It is vital to know your Win Rate because it is your Win Rate and the size of your wagers that will determine your potential net winnings. These two factors hold the key to a much larger bank account. *Beginning capital* is the amount of money that you set aside at the beginning of each year[12] to use for sports wagering. Knowing your beginning capital is the cornerstone to managing your money and controlling risk. We will discuss risk control and money management later in the book.

Continuing on with the Scorecard, the returns get even more compelling when you start with more beginning capital. In Scorecard 1.2, we assume that instead of starting with $1,000 and making $50 wagers, you start with $10,000 and make wagers of $500 on each game. As in the first example, we will also assume that you make 20 wagers per week:

Scorecard 1.2

- **$10,000 beginning capital**

- **20 wagers per week ($500 wagers per game)**

Win Rate	Net Annual Winnings
60%	$ 80,000
65%	$132,500
70%	$185,000
75%	$237,500
80%	$290,000
85%	$342,500

Wow, Scorecard 1.2 tells us that we can earn $80,000 annually on $10,000 of beginning capital if we have a Win Rate of just 60 percent.

---

12 A betting year does not have to be a calendar year. You might start at the beginning of a particular sports season, or you can simply start randomly on any given date. Allocating your beginning capital is discussed in detail Chapter Eight.

That means that at the end of the year, we'll have $90,000 — the beginning investment of $10,000 plus our $80,000 of winnings.

So what makes me think you can win 60 percent of your bets, anyway? Isn't that overly optimistic? Not if you know what you're doing. Remember, sensible sports wagering using the *Get In and Win* System is not a coin toss. By definition you have more than an average chance of winning because you are an informed, serious bettor, not some well-intentioned chump rooting for the home team or blindly following the odds given by a sports book. As mentioned previously, a 60 percent Win Rate means that you win six out of every 10 bets. Football and basketball teams that win six games out of every 10 are viewed as just above average. But in sports wagering, being just above average can earn you a lot — if you have the discipline to systematically repeat the process over and over again. As Scorecard 1.2 tells us, a 60 percent Win Rate means $80,000 per year with beginning capital of $10,000 — and you only have to put 5 percent of your investment at risk on each game! Diversification is a common risk management technique on Wall Street. Five-percent positions diversify your bets just enough to maximize profits when you correctly pick the winners, while avoiding the wipeout when you are wrong.

In the NFL, a 60 percent Win Rate gets you a record of 9-7 (sometimes 10-6), a wild card berth and a likely early exit in the playoffs. Do you think Bill Belichick approaches each season as if his New England Patriots are going to be just above average and finish a 9-7 team? Read on.

The Power of Thinking Like Bill Belichick

Let's see what happens when we start to think like Bill Belichick. He begins every season with the goal of making it to the Super Bowl. He knows that to give his team the best opportunity to make a run at the Super Bowl, the Patriots need to win their division so that they can secure home field advantage throughout the playoffs. To accomplish these goals, he knows that his team must likely win at least 12 games during the regular season; that's a winning percentage of 75 percent of games played — a reasonable expectation for a good football team.

Now let's go back to our Scorecards and approach sports wagering as if we were Bill Belichick. With that in mind, we would do all that we could to prepare ourselves to have a Win Rate of 75 percent. When we look at our Scorecard 1.2, we see that a Win Rate of 75 percent in the sports wagering markets can result in annual winnings to us of approximately $23,750 if we start with $1,000 of beginning capital, and an astounding $237,500 annually if we start with $10,000. Wagering on sports the way Bill Belichick approaches a football season can really be rewarding.

The Math Works Big-Time

Let's look at two more Scorecards and see what we could earn if we expect the same kind of win-loss record from ourselves as we do from very good sports teams. Let's say we have a two-year time horizon to build a real winner, and that because we are just starting out, our beginning capital is limited to $5,000. Let's also say we expect to have 20 games or wagers per week and that in the first year, again because we are just starting out, we anticipate that out of every 20 games we will win 12 games and lose eight. That means we will have a Win Rate of 60 percent — a little above average.

But just like Bill Belichick, our goal is to build a *real* winner, so we are going to focus and work really, really hard. For Year Two, we are going to suppose our Win Rate improves to 70 percent (because we are becoming even smarter bettors), and we continue to wager on 20 games a week. Further, let's assume that we take all of our winnings and our initial capital investment from the first year and roll it over to the second year. Because we want to maximize our profits while protecting against downside losses, we will practice prudent risk management and size our wagers at a constant 5 percent of our initial capital. Now, let's run the numbers and see where we would end up at the end of our second year:

Scorecard 1.3

- **Year 1**

- **$5,000 beginning capital**

- **20 wagers per week ($250 wagers per game)**

Win Rate	Net Annual Winnings
60%	$ 40,000
65%	$ 66,250
70%	$ 92,500
75%	$118,750
80%	$145,000
85%	$171,250

Scorecard 1.4

- **Year 2**

- **$45,000 beginning capital**

- **20 wagers per week ($2,250 wagers per game)**

Win Rate	Net Annual Winnings
60%	$ 360,000
65%	$ 596,250
70%	$ 832.500
75%	$1,068,750
80%	$1,305,000
85%	$1,541,250

Scorecards 1.3 and 1.4 show us what would happen if we were able to achieve a 60 percent Win Rate in Year One and then, with the benefit of our first-year experience, we increase our Win Rate to 70 percent in Year Two. By reinvesting our Year One winnings plus our beginning capital (a total of $45,000) and increasing our Year Two Win Rate to 70 percent, we would have approximately $837,500 at the end of Year Two — all on an original investment of just $5,000!

Mark Teixeira and Warren Buffett Make the Big Money; So Can You

Now, let's say that again. Assuming you start with capital of $5,000 and you accomplish the same goals as you would in building a winning sports team, the Scorecard calculations show that you can earn $832,500 over a two-year period. I'll admit that this may seem too good to be true, so let's put what you can earn in context. We are dealing in the world of sports, where Larry Fitzgerald, a wide receiver for the Arizona Cardinals, recently signed an eight-year contract extension for approximately $120 million; Mark Teixeira, a first baseman, recently signed a six-year contract with the New York Yankees for $175 million; and John Calipari, the basketball coach at the University of Kentucky, received a new contract worth $36.5 million that runs through the 2018-19 season. There is money being made in professional and college sports — a lot of money — and the *Get In and Win* System will show you how to get your share.

The key is to understand that the very same statistical models, contrarian strategies and valuation principles that successful investors like Warren Buffett and others on Wall Street use to make millions of dollars can be applied to sports wagering. But to make money, you need the right mathematical and money management tools. Don't worry — you needn't be a math or finance whiz to win at sports betting, because I've done most of the heavy lifting for you. The *Get In and Win* System focuses your attention on the numbers and facts that matter — giving you the opportunity to apply your own sports knowledge to win more bets than you lose.

All that remains is for you to approach sports betting just the way the Patriots get ready for each football season. They start by establishing a goal, then go about achieving it through hard work, preparation and discipline. Said another way, you can risk $5,000 and invest the time and effort required to earn $832,500 over a two-year period, or you can have no plan and wind up like the NBA's hapless Los Angeles Clippers. It all depends on your preparation and commitment to winning the game.

A Sports Book: The New York Stock Exchange of Sports Wagering

Chances are pretty good that if you are reading this book you are fairly serious about sports. As a serious fan, you follow all your favorite teams and players with keen interest. You may have already played in a fantasy sports league, participated in March Madness bracket mania, and perhaps even placed a bet or two on a team or a game that you knew well. You are interested in taking your sports knowledge and insights into the games to the next level.

That level is called a sports book. A sports book is simply a financial market, just like the stock, foreign exchange or commodity markets. It's a place where the prices assigned to financial instruments (or teams) are posted, and money is exchanged at the stated price. Just as the New York Stock Exchange is a market for financial instruments, a sports book is a market for the outcome of sporting events. In fact, many Wall Street market makers refer to their portfolio positions as their *book*. The price quoted to transact a monetary exchange on the outcome of a sporting event is called a *line*. The lines are the prices posted by the sports book.

At first glance, the information posted in a sports book seems overwhelming and confusing. It reminds me of the first time I picked up *The Wall Street Journal* as a teenager and saw all of that eye-glazing financial information. But eventually, with training and experience, I was able to breeze through the financial data with the same ease with which I read the box scores in the sports section. In subsequent chapters, we will defog the sports book's crystal ball — exploring in detail what all the postings mean as well as explaining how they operate. All you need to know for now is that once you understand them, sports books are easy for you to access and use. They are open 24 hours a day, seven days a week and have all the real-time information you could possibly want about your favorite teams and players. For the serious sports fan, applying the lessons of the *Get In and Win* System at a sports book can lead to the fulfillment of a dream.

2

The Sports Betting Game

To get a handle on how sports betting works — and how you can win — imagine it as a game involving six players and officiated by one referee. The players are Amateur Andy, Streaking Steve, Louie the Loser, Last Chance Vance, Frank the Fan and you, the Intelligent Bettor. We will refer to the referee as Leonard the Line Maker. The game is played at a sports book. The referee, Leonard, has a very important job with a lot of responsibilities. Like any good official, Leonard must ensure the integrity of the game and make sure all the players observe the rules. But the most important thing that Leonard does is establish the point spread or set the line for each game.

The Point Spread

The most common type of sports betting proposition is the point spread wager. Sports books present a football point spread wager or a betting line as follows:

```
Dallas
New England     -7
```

This line is spoken as "New England minus seven." It tells us that Dallas is the visiting team because Dallas' name appears on the top. Of more importance, it tells us New England (the team favored to win) is giving 7 points and that Dallas (the underdog) is getting 7 points.[13] Since New England is giving 7 points, it must win the game by 8 points or more for a bet on New England to pay off. On the other hand, since Dallas is getting 7 points, it must lose by 6 points or less, or win outright, for a bet on Dallas to pay off. If New England wins the game by exactly 7 points, no one wins and no one loses. That is called a *push*, and everyone who wagered gets his money back.

The point spread can be viewed as a handicap given to the team favored to win the game. Therefore, when you wager on a favorite, you are giving (or "laying") points. When you bet on an underdog, you are taking or receiving points. The point spread theoretically makes any game an equal proposition on the sports betting market, no matter how great the actual mismatch between the two teams might seem to be. The purpose of the point spread is to equally divide the amount of money wagered on the game, so that the amount bet on Dallas is the same as the amount bet on New England.

A slight variation on the point spread is the half point. This represents adding or subtracting a half point from a whole number. For example, -7 points in our example might be changed to -6.5 or -7.5. The half point, commonly referred to as *the hook*, was devised to eliminate pushes and convert them to wins or losses. It can also be used as a device for the sports book to balance the books, as discussed below.

Sports Books: The Games Are Played Here

Legal sports betting takes place at a variety of sports books located around the globe and on hundreds of websites, assuming you are located somewhere that allows such betting. When referencing sports books, we are talking about companies that are authorized to do business in the countries

---

13 Some not familiar with sports betting find it counterintuitive that the team with a negative number next to its name (in this instance, New England) is the team the sports betting public expects to win the game. If you are one of those that find this confusing, simply remember to subtract the number of "minus points" from the favored team's final score to determine the winner of the wager.

where they operate — some of them are publicly traded on the global financial markets — not local bookies. In the U.S., the most popular sports books are in Las Vegas and are located in large casinos like the Bellagio, the Mandalay Bay and Bally's. Sports books provide the venue and mechanism for our friend Leonard the Line Maker to set his prices and post the lines.

Sports books also provide all the financial systems necessary to record and settle the wagers. Sports betting is a zero-sum game, meaning that for every dollar won there is a dollar lost. The losers pay the winners and the winners pay the sports books out of their profits. Unlike casino blackjack and poker games, in which the house actually bets, all the money cycling through a sports book comes from the individual bettors; the sports book merely acts as a financial intermediary, taking a fee for processing the transactions.

As such, sports books operate very much like the commodity and option exchanges in the financial markets. In the commodity market, players — or traders, as they are known — buy and sell futures contracts. A simple example would be a basic oil futures contract. Let's assume that there is someone who believes oil prices will exceed $80 per barrel six months from now and is willing to pay a certain amount today for the right to buy the oil for something less than $80 per barrel in six months. His hope is to profit when oil prices rise, since he can then buy it for less. In the world of finance, that is described as buying a call option on a futures contract. On the other side of this trade is someone who is equally convinced that oil will be selling way below $80 per barrel six months from now. He is willing to sell a call option today at a price that he believes will be relatively high in six months — because he is convinced oil will be selling for *less* than the option price.

If at the end of six months the price of oil is above $80 per barrel, the buyer of the call option wins. If the price is below $80 per barrel, the seller of the call option wins. But in no instance can both win, because it is a zero-sum game. Commodity futures are traded all over the world, but the best-known venue is the Chicago Board of Trade's Options Exchange. Such exchanges act very much like a referee in a sporting event. They make sure the game of options trading is played fairly, keep the score, and receive a fee or commission for officiating.

Sports betting is no different. As an example, let's take the line on the professional football game introduced at the beginning of this chapter between the Dallas Cowboys and the New England Patriots. The line on the game is New England -7. That means New England (the favorite) must win the game by more than 7 points for those betting on New England to win their bet. More importantly, -7 points is theoretically the price, or odds, on the game that the sports book must post to ensure that there is an equal amount of money wagered on the Cowboys and the Patriots. A bet on the Patriots is essentially buying a call option that New England will win by more than 7 points. A bet on Dallas is like selling the call option, with the belief that either Dallas wins outright or New England wins by less than 7 points. After the game is played, there will be a winner and a loser on the Dallas-versus–New England proposition. Either way, the sports book collects a fee to make sure all the trades are settled.

The Commission: A Success Fee

In point spread wagering, a sports book typically pays out $10 in winnings for each $11 wagered. What this means is that when you place a wager on Dallas and want to win $100, you must put down $110. If you want to win $50, you must put $55 at risk. And if you want to win $1,000, you must make a bet of $1,100.[14] Let's say two bettors wager $110 on opposite sides of the same point spread, meaning $110 is wagered on Dallas and $110 is wagered on New England, so the sports book collects $220. Assuming the actual outcome of game is not a *push* (meaning New England does not win by exactly 7 points), then one bettor wins and the other bettor loses. The winner receives a total of $210 — the $110 he put at risk and the $100 profit from a winning wager. That leaves the sports book with its commission or fee of $10. This $10 fee is also sometimes called *vigorish* or just *vig*. The term *vigorish* derives from the Russian *vyigrysh*, meaning "winnings" or "profit from gambling," and was brought to America early

---

14 As a matter of convenience, most bettors wager in even $10 increments. For example, a $10 wager wins $9.10; a $50 wager wins $45.50; a $100 wager wins $91; and a $1,000 wager wins $910.

in the 20th century by speakers of Yiddish. No matter what it's called, let's be sure to note who paid the sports book. It was the winner, not the loser.

The winner pays the commission because without the services of the sports book, the winnings would have been $110 — the same as the amount wagered. Instead, the winner collected only $100 profit. So the winner won approximately 91 percent of what he stood to lose, and the sports book collected a 9 percent commission. While that may seem steep, it's the cost of doing business. It may make you feel better if you think of the commission as a *success fee* that you pay only if you win.

Remember the Scorecards we discussed in the previous chapter? They showed how there were loads of money to be made, even after paying out the success fee, so don't get hung up on the amount of the commission. Often it does pay to shop around among the various sports books, because there are times when reduced fees are offered as an incentive to do business. But the bottom line is to stay focused on winning your wagers, even if you decide to minimize your transaction costs by shopping among several sports books for the best value.

Balancing the Books

What do accountants and sports books have in common? They both want the books to balance. Sports books are in business to collect fees for providing a venue where sports wagers are made, and to facilitate the settlement process, not to make a bet on who will win or lose a game. *Their sole function is to act as an impartial broker that receives a fee for providing a service.* You should always remember that key fact; it means that sports books do not have an opinion about the outcome of the game. Their operators only want to be sure that an equal amount is wagered on either side of the betting line. The primary device the sports book uses for balancing the books is the point spread. This is very important to keep in mind, because it means that the point spread is *not* a prediction of the outcome of the game. It is simply a handicap applied to the favorite to make certain that the wagering action is divided equally between the favorite and the underdog.

Why is that equality so important to the sports book? Because if the wagering isn't divided equally, the sports book is exposed to a loss — that is, they could conceivably have to pay out more than they take in. So when the sports book sees that more money is being wagered on New England than Dallas, it will adjust the point spread slightly to restore the balance. It might move New England to -7.5 to discourage wagering on New England and encourage wagering on Dallas. With equal amounts of money bet on each team, the sports book is assured a profit from its commissions. The best betting line from the sports book's perspective is one that allows for balanced wagering on both teams from the time it is posted until the time the game is played.

Leonard the Line Maker

Imagine that the point spread or line for any particular sporting event as being set by a remarkably accommodating and fair-minded referee named Leonard the Line Maker. Leonard is efficient, diligent and laser-focused. He is committed to his primary responsibility of balancing the books in an objective and dispassionate way. He has no favorites among the teams playing in the games and he has no opinion as to the outcomes. He simply wants to balance the action.

Without fail, Leonard appears daily and names the prices at which you can wager on one team or the other in each of the professional and major college games to be played that day. Even though Leonard is a very stable fellow, his quotations will be anything but. That's because Leonard is simply a pawn of public opinion. So when the consensus view for a team is favorable, he adds considerably to the point spread and sets a very high number. At other times, when the public can see nothing but trouble ahead for a particular team, he must be very accommodating and post an enticing number to attract some action on that team.

Leonard has another endearing characteristic. He doesn't mind being ignored. If his point spread is uninteresting to you today, he will be back with a new one tomorrow. Wagers are strictly at your option. You are free to either ignore him or take advantage of him, but it will be disastrous for you if you fall under his influence, as many less intelligent bettors do. His job is to serve you, not to guide you.

Now that we've met Leonard, let's meet the six players in the game of sports betting.

Amateur Andy

Andy is the typical amateur bettor who wagers only on his favorite teams — a terrible mistake. And to make matters worse, he usually bets on the public favorites — teams that *everyone* loves and sees as infallible. He doesn't realize that 80 percent of people (although not 80 percent of the money bet on the game) wager almost exclusively on favorites. This is especially true of the most popular teams, like the Cowboys, the Patriots, the Yankees and the Red Sox, the Lakers, and college teams like Notre Dame football and Duke basketball. Andy doesn't understand the heavy tariff that he pays as a result of his belief in the superior team.

Andy is unaware that when Leonard the Line Maker sees a team attracting a lot of betting action, Leonard has no choice but to add one, two or even three points to the spread. Leonard does this to inflict the maximum pain on the favored team's bettors and to encourage more wagers on the underdog. Despite the point spread edge the underdog receives, Andy continues to ignore the extra points that he must pay to play the favorites. He lacks the self-confidence to risk his money on the team no one else wants. So he follows the crowd. By the time the game rolls around, Andy is often paying such a high premium that the odds are stacked against him before the game even begins.

Streaking Steve

Steve is a very excitable type. He loves sports and is totally engaged in sports betting. He reads all the newspapers, watches ESPN daily, and surfs the Web looking for information that will give him an advantage. But boy, can he get excited, especially when he gets on a winning streak. When

Steve hits a few winners in a row, he just can't control himself. And this is where he makes his big mistake. He violates one of the essential principles of successful sports betting: He starts increasing his bet sizes with each consecutive win.

As his winning streak gains momentum, Steve claims he can "feel the power," and he lets his winnings ride. That is, if his standard bet is $100 and he wins, he rolls the winnings of $92 in with his beginning capital of $100 and makes a $192 wager on the next game. If he wins again, his next bet is $368. After each win, he doubles down the next time. He just can't bring himself to take any money off the table because he has convinced himself that he is the chosen one. But somewhere out there, a pin lies waiting to burst his bubble. Inevitably, all his winnings, as well as his beginning capital, disappear like home runs from AT&T Park into the San Francisco Bay. But Steve continues undeterred until his pockets are empty and he can bet no more.

Louie the Loser

Louie is either ill-informed or lazy. He isn't willing to do his homework and is overconfident. He bets in a helter-skelter manner, with no game plan or money management system in place. He gets the bright idea one day that he will get rich quick betting on sports, although he doesn't have a basic understanding of probability theory. He is a self-described expert because he watches a couple of games on the weekend. He may even be successful in some other business or profession, and he thinks that achievement automatically guarantees sports betting profits. He bets based on gut instinct or some other half-baked program that has no mathematical basis.

Louie wants to strike it rich with one big bet. He wants bang for his buck, so he plays the long odds looking for the big payoff. As a result, he recklessly bets the parlays, the teasers and other exotic wagers where there is little chance of winning.[15] He lives for the action and makes lots of bets

---

15 I'll dissect those bets in Chapter Ten.

every day without regard to value. Louie has no patience or discipline. His quest for the big payoff will lead to the big payout.

Last Chance Vance

Poor Vance — he could be a successful bettor. He does everything right. He keeps it simple. He understands how to calculate and find value. He makes only high-percentage bets. He has a good money management system. He does his homework and is willing to grind out profits slowly over time by diversifying his bets. Vance has all the right things going for him, except he has one fatal flaw. He panics when he hits a short-term losing streak.

Here is a familiar pattern for Vance: He bets $100 each on 12 college football games on Saturday, and then be bets $100 each on eight NFL games on Sunday. Unfortunately, even though he has been disciplined in his approach through the weekend, Vance has had one of those weekends that all bettors inevitably encounter. In short, things have not gone his way, and he finds himself down $250. So instead of regrouping, confident that he will make it up next week, he panics and abandons his prudent money management plan. Vance decides to make it all up on the Monday Night Football game, so he doubles down. In order to turn a profit for the week, he bets the $250 that he is in the hole plus an additional $250, for a total of $500, on that one game. He loses. Vance has turned a small-loss weekend into a disaster.

Frank the Fan

No one can fault Frank. He is a "homey" and loves his favorite teams. He bets a modest amount of money on his local heroes each week because it increases his interest and enjoyment of the games. In placing his wagers, he pays little or no attention to the point spread because he is a devoted fan. His home-team bias is even more pronounced when it comes to betting on games involving his college alma mater. Frank bets with his heart and not his head. His primary motivation is his love for the home teams.

The Intelligent Bettor

The Intelligent Bettor knows that sports wagering is most successful when it is conducted in a businesslike way. For him, that means his bets are placed using a disciplined approach based on sound arithmetic, not just a vague feeling of optimism. He has a systematic approach that he can apply consistently over and over again to grind out profits. He understands that the first rule of making money is not to lose it, so he seeks a Margin of Safety[16] in his wagers to mitigate risk. He has a good understanding of mathematical probabilities and takes a disciplined approach to money management.

Because the Intelligent Bettor has done his homework, he has confidence in his information, knowledge and judgment. He is a contrarian — he doesn't follow the crowd and is not influenced by Leonard's point spreads. He knows that the best moneymaking opportunities are found when his assessment of a bet differs significantly from the line that Leonard posts. When he sees a difference, he has the courage to act on it and not hesitate.

The Intelligent Bettor knows that Leonard the Line Maker is only a referee and that the point spread Leonard posts is only the number required to balance the books. He does not interpret the point spread as a prediction of the outcome of the game. He is aware that he is playing a game against Amateur Andy, Streaking Steve, Louie the Loser, Last Chance Vance and Frank the Fan. The Intelligent Bettor recognizes Andy, Steve, Louie, Vance and Frank for what they are, but he harbors no ill will toward them. Quite the opposite: He is grateful for their wagers, which will soon be in *his* pocket. Above his computer he has posted his favorite quote, from Mark Twain: "Let us be thankful for the fools; but for them the rest of us could not succeed."

---

16 The Margin of Safety concept is described in great detail in Chapter Four.

Getting Started — The Fundamentals

Winning money — lots of it — wagering on sports happens every day, but only for a few. And what do those winners all have in common? They have the proper mind-set. They are contrarians — meaning that they are willing to go against the public consensus when the odds and potential payoff are in their favor. John Maynard Keynes, the celebrated British economist, once said, "Worldly wisdom teaches that it is better for one's reputation to fail conventionally than to succeed unconventionally." Taking the opposite view, a contrarian feels comfortable rejecting the good reputation that can come with conventional failure. A contrarian embraces what it takes to run against the crowd, motivated by the great rewards that await him if he wins the race down the path less traveled.

While being a contrarian is desirable, the simple act of being a contrarian by itself will not make you an Intelligent Bettor and bring you riches. If you are in a movie theater that catches on fire, you would be well advised to ignore your contrarian instincts and leave the theater with the rest of the audience. In the same way, successful sports betting is not about automatically going against public opinion. It's about using the *Get In and Win* System to identify when the consensus opinion about a game appears to be wrong — and then acting to profit from the misperception. Being a contrarian is an important attribute of an Intelligent Bettor, but it is not the whole job. It will only get you part of the way there.

The other piece of the puzzle is being able to identify value — with value being defined as the gap between the posted line and the most likely outcome of a game. On Wall Street, a valuation gap between the actual worth of a security and the market price is called a mispricing. A mispricing occurs when Coca-Cola shares worth $65 are trading at $55. Finding value is the purpose of the *Get In and Win* System. Once *Get In and Win* has identified a mispricing, the Intelligent Bettor trusts his contrarian instincts and acts decisively to profit from the valuation gap, because without action all that remains are missed opportunities and that empty feeling you get when you reach into your pockets and find nothing there.

The Line Maker Is Not Your Enemy

Remember from Chapter Two that Leonard the Line Maker's objective is to get an equal amount wagered on each team. For him, setting the point spread is about anticipating how people will bet, as opposed to determining what the final score will actually be. Thus, despite what many bettors think, Leonard's point spread is not a prediction of the outcome of the game.

To see what a point spread *is*, rather than what most people *think it is*, let's look at the opening spread posted on the 1993 Super Bowl between the Dallas Cowboys and the Buffalo Bills. Dallas opened as a 7.5-point favorite and wound up winning the game in a rout, 52-17. The opening point spread missed the mark by a whopping 27.5 points. After the game, there was plenty of criticism directed at the line maker and the sports books — about how "wrong" they had been in assessing the outcome of the game. In reality, the opening line was indeed incorrect, but the line was *not too low at all*. In fact, the 7.5-point opening line turned out to be *too high*. The opening line was too high because a large number of bettors who thought the Bills were going to cover — either by winning the game outright or at least losing by less than 7.5 points — started to wager heavily on the Bills. With a disproportionate amount of money flowing in on Buffalo, the sports books found themselves at risk and were forced to make betting on the Cowboys a more attractive proposition. The point spread that opened at

7.5 was moved down to 7, then to 6.5, then 6, and at some sports books the line went as low as 5.5 as Leonard and his colleagues at competing sports books struggled to encourage more wagering on the Cowboys so they could balance the amount bet on each team. In the end, Dallas won the game by a lot more than the point spread, leaving those who had bet so heavily on Buffalo with nothing in their wallets.

The Contrarian Versus the Competition

The Intelligent Bettor knows that the point spread merely represents the consensus opinion of the general betting public, which gives him a good look at what the betting competition is thinking. The competition is represented by the people we met in Chapter Two: Amateur Andy, Streaking Steve, Louie the Loser, Last Chance Vance and Frank the Fan. The Intelligent Bettor knows that he is pitting his judgment against the collective feelings of the general public, not against an expert with more or better information. Leonard the Line Maker is only balancing their wagers.

Andy, Steve, Louie, Vance and Frank, because of their personal biases, are not betting intelligently. They represent dumb money. And it is precisely because the point spread is meant to balance this dumb money that sports betting becomes a winnable proposition. Anyone willing to take the time to formulate an informed contrarian approach and become an Intelligent Bettor will have an obvious advantage. The question is not whether you can outsmart the experts. The question is whether you can outsmart Andy, Steve, Louie, Vance and Frank (most of the time). This is not rocket science!

The Five Essentials for Successful Sports Betting

In addition to a contrarian mind-set, there are five essentials that you must have to win consistently and earn profits when betting on sports. They are:

1. A better model
2. Superior information
3. Risk control through selective betting
4. Careful money management
5. Discipline

Before we dive into the details of these fundamentals in subsequent chapters, let's get a general understanding of what they mean and why they are important.

1. A Better Model: *Get In and Win*

The first requirement for placing winning bets is a better wagering model — that is, a framework for analyzing and betting on a game that gives you an edge over what other bettors are doing. You want a process that is accurate and easy to use. And because there are lots of potential games to analyze each day, you need something that can be applied over and over again in a time-efficient way. The *Get In and Win* System incorporates all of these elements. It produces profitable results. Its elegance is in its simplicity. It is a systematic approach. And it requires a minimum amount of time to maintain and apply to each game. The *Get In and Win* System is that better model you have been looking for, because it puts the odds in your favor.

Sometimes it is better to be lucky than good, but over time it is better to be good than lucky. In too many cases, bettors dwell solely on outcomes without appropriate consideration of process. The focus on results is to some degree understandable. Results — whether it's the final numbers on the scoreboard in a game or the bottom-line net earnings in a business — are what ultimately matter. And results are typically easier to evaluate than processes. But the Intelligent Bettor knows that a well-executed process leads to the results that will make his bank account bigger.

Paul DePodesta, a baseball executive and a key member of Billy Beane's brain trust with the Oakland A's, tells a story in *Moneyball* about playing blackjack in Las Vegas. A card player to DePodesta's right, sitting on 17, asked for a hit. Everyone at the table gasped, and even the dealer asked the player if he was sure. The player nodded yes, and the dealer, to everyone's surprise, turned over a four. The gambler had a perfect hand. "Nice hit," said the dealer. As DePodesta points out, it was indeed a great hit, but it was also a very lucky hit. Calling for a card when you're sitting on 17 almost always ends up as a losing hand for the player and a moneymaker for the house — which is why the dealer complimented the rash gambler, no doubt hoping he would press his *dumb* luck even further, so the house could win back its losses.

A good process must be trusted even when it occasionally fails (and it will). Sports bettors, like blackjack players, often make the critical mistake of assuming that a good process always yields good outcomes and that bad outcomes imply a bad process. By contrast, the most successful performers in any field where probabilities matter — such as investing, sports team management, coaching and sports wagering — *all emphasize the process over the outcome*, because they know that with the gift of time, a good process applied consistently will produce winning results.

At the heart of the *Get In and Win* System is a simple matrix that Michael Mausboussin, a Wall Street investment banker, uses to illustrate the process-versus-outcome message. The matrix shows that because of luck, good decisions will sometimes lead to bad outcomes, and bad decisions will sometimes lead to good outcomes — as the hit-on-17 story above illustrates. But over the long haul, a good process will always prevail.

PROCESS versus OUTCOME			
		Outcome	
		Good	Bad
Process Used to Make the Decision	Good	Deserved Success	Bad Break
	Bad	Dumb Luck	Poetic Justice

The Intelligent Bettor understands this matrix and is confident that over time, more thoughtful decision-making will lead to better overall results, and more thoughtful decision-making can be encouraged by evaluating decisions on how well they were made rather than based solely on their outcome.

2. Superior Information: See the Invisible Gorilla

Every winning sports bettor needs superior information. This is not to be confused with *more* information. Facts and stats about professional and college sports teams are available everywhere, from daily newspapers to thousands of websites. We often believe more information provides more clarity and improves our decision-making. But in reality, additional information often just serves to confuse the decision-making process. In the investment business, the best investors know that the incremental knowledge gained can actually decrease with each additional piece of information added.

James Montier, an expert financial analyst and a partner in the well-respected investment firm GMO, says it this way in his book *Value Investing*: "Often in the investment business, which has an obsession with minutia, too much time is spent trying to find out more and more about less and less, until we know everything about nothing. Rarely, if ever, do we stop and ask ourselves what we actually need to know!" Along that line, it may be interesting cocktail party chatter to know how many bottles of Coca-Cola are sold worldwide, but when it comes down to valuing Coca-Cola's stock price, it is earnings per share (not bottles sold) that counts. So whether you are investing in stocks or betting on sports, more information is not necessarily better.

What matters to sports bettors is information that helps determine who will win a game, and by how many points. Nothing else is relevant. The *Get In and Win* System focuses your attention on those statistics that are important to placing winning bets, allowing you to disregard the vast ocean of statistics in every sport that are of little or no betting value. A systematic process for evaluating information is required because our ability to focus is often imperfect, a fact that both magicians and scientists have known for years.

Diagram 3.1

In his book *Stumbling on Happiness*, renowned Harvard psychologist Daniel Gilbert describes a memory assessment involving the six royal cards that appear in Diagram 3.1. Like Gilbert, I ask you to look at the six cards in Diagram 3.1 and pick your favorite. No, don't tell me. Keep it to yourself. Just look at the card, and say the name once or twice (or write it down) so that you will remember it in a page or so.

Now moving away from the cards for a moment, let's consider how scientists identified the problem they call "attention blindness." In *Stumbling on Happiness*, Gilbert details an experiment that could have been taken straight from the pages of the television show *Candid Camera*. In the experiment, Daniel Simons, a professor at the University of Illinois, arranged for researchers to approach pedestrians on a college campus and ask for directions to a particular building. While the pedestrian and the researcher conferred over the researcher's map, two construction workers, each holding one end of a large door, rudely cut between them, temporarily obstructing the pedestrian's view of the researcher. As the construction workers passed, the original researcher crouched behind the door and walked off with the construction workers, while a new researcher, who had been hiding behind the door all along, took his place and picked up the conversation. The original and substitute researcher were of different heights and builds and had noticeably different voices, haircuts and clothing. You would have no trouble telling them apart if they were standing side by side. So what did the Good Samaritans who stopped to help a seemingly lost tourist make of this switcheroo? Not much. In fact, most of the pedestrians failed to notice that the person to whom they were talking had suddenly been transformed into an entirely new individual.

Later, while teaching at Harvard in the late 1990s, Simon, along with one of his students, Christopher Chabris, came up with another innovative idea to test how the brain processes information. Now famous, their 60-second experiment, known as the Invisible Gorilla, was outrageously simple — it required only that you watch a video of six students passing a basketball. Three were dressed in black and three in white. Viewers were asked to count the number of times the players in white passed the ball to each other as they rotated in a circle, while simultaneously weaving between the players in black. During the video, a woman in a full-body gorilla suit walked into the center of the frame, pounded her chest and then walked off, spending nine seconds on the screen. Shockingly, about half the people who took the test — in countless airings of the video all over the world — did not notice the woman in the gorilla suit. If you haven't seen this video, it is definitely worth watching.[17] Some who didn't see the woman dressed as a gorilla protested that the video had been rigged. People who did see her were incredulous: How could so many miss something so obvious? This experiment reveals two things: that we are missing a lot of what goes on around us, and that we have no idea that we are missing so much. In fact George Miller, one of the most notable psychologists of the 20th century, found that the average human's conscious memory can handle just seven bits of information, plus or minus two.[18]

But long before scientists Gilbert, Simon, Chabris and Miller performed their studies, Sir Arthur Conan Doyle had the ever insightful Sherlock Holmes explain to his readers: "I consider that a man's brain originally is like an empty attic, and he gets to stock it with the furniture of his choice. A fool takes in all the lumber of every sort that he comes across, so that the knowledge which might be useful to him gets crowded out, or at best is jumbled up with a lot of other things, so that he has difficulty laying his

---

17 The video can be viewed at www.invisiblegorilla.com. To have even more fun, test it on a friend.

18 Miller's article "The Magic Number Seven, Plus or Minus Two" was published in the *Psychological Review* in 1956.

hands on it. But the skillful workman is very careful indeed as to what he takes into his brain-attic. He will have nothing but the tools which may help him in doing his work, but of these he has a large assortment, and all in all in the most perfect order. He knows there will come a time when for every addition of knowledge you forget something you knew before. It is of the highest importance, therefore, not to have useless facts elbowing out the useful ones."

Of course, magicians have known this for centuries. Returning to Gilbert's card test, a few pages back you chose a card from a group of six. What I didn't tell you at the time was that Gilbert and I have powers far beyond those of mortal men, and therefore I knew which card you were going to pick before you picked it. To prove it, I have removed your card from the group. Take a look at Diagram 3.2 and tell me I'm not amazing.

Diagram 3.2

How did I do it? Well, the trick is much more entertaining when you don't know beforehand that it is a trick. And it doesn't work at all if you compare the two diagrams side by side, because you instantly see that none of the cards in Diagram 3.1 are in Diagram 3.2!

While these examples may be entertaining, what's most important to note is how easily we can be distracted. And when we do get sidetracked, we miss the obvious. It is precisely for this reason that professional investors and analysts, recognizing that their perception of information can often be skewed, use a disciplined, systematic approach (consistently applied) to focus their attention on information that is relevant to the investment process. *Get In and Win*'s step-by-step approach will provide you with the insight necessary to focus on the stats and facts that matter, giving you an informed edge over the other bettors. With *Get In and Win*, you will learn to view sports information in an entirely new way so that you won't miss the Invisible Gorilla in the room or be fooled by an amateur magician's card tricks.

3. Controlling Risk: Don't Swing at Every Pitch

Risk can be defined as that which interferes with an intended result. In the case of sports betting, the intended result is simply winning a high percentage of the wagers you place. In life and in sports betting, risk and uncertainty are inevitable, and there is nothing positive about them. The Intelligent Bettor is constantly aware of risk, and always seeking to avoid it. No one wants to lose his sports wagering capital. Just as on Wall Street, risk cannot be completely eliminated in betting on sports, but it can be managed and controlled.

The primary risk management tool in the Intelligent Bettor's toolbox is selectivity. The Intelligent Bettor guards against risk of loss by placing wagers only on those games where he believes he has a real advantage. He keeps his wagers focused, and he passes on a lot of possible bets. He doesn't feel any pressure to bet on every game. He has done his homework; he trusts his model for analyzing the game; and he acts when he sees that the odds are in his favor. The Intelligent Bettor places a bet the way Ted Williams approached hitting a baseball.

Williams was one of the greatest hitters in baseball history. He combined power (521 lifetime home runs) with patience (more walks than any other player of his era) and control (a .344 lifetime batting average). He documented his legacy in a thesis on batting titled *The Science of Hitting* — a book that characterized hitting as a real-life application of geometry. Williams explained that when entering the batter's box he would mentally divide the strike zone into a quadrant made up of 77 color-coded compartments all equal in size (each compartment was the size of a baseball). He also assigned a number for what he thought his batting average would be when pitches were thrown in each of those 77 discrete areas.

Williams wrote that he would only swing at pitches that were in those compartments where he knew he could usually connect and get a hit a high percentage of the time. If a pitch was on the fringe, he would patiently wait for the next pitch. He knew that a called strike was better than swinging at a bad pitch, which could result in an out. Moreover, there were only *three* areas where he thought he would hit .400 — talk about a picky hitter! In 1941, Williams became the last major leaguer to hit over .400 for an entire season (.406).

The great thing about sports betting is that there are no called strikes. You can stand at the plate and let the pitcher (our friend Leonard the Line Maker) throw pitch after pitch right down the middle, and you don't have to swing! If the "pitch" he's throwing is New England -7 and you don't know enough to decide on that bet, you can let it go right by. There is no umpire to call a strike. In sports betting, taking a swing is entirely at your discretion. If only it were so easy for Ted Williams! For you, there is only one way to strike out, and that's if you swing and miss, so there is no reason to swing unless you see the pitch you want. The *Get In and Win* System will show you how to selectivity identify the fat pitches where there is a Margin of Safety, which is discussed in the next chapter.

4. Careful Money Management: Crank Out the Singles

The first rule of making money is don't lose it. While we know that losses are inevitable, it is vital to control them in order to protect your sports betting capital. One way you can do this is to limit the size of your wagers. Wagering a consistent 5 percent of your investment capital will properly balance your wagers, enhance your returns and limit the amount that you can lose on any one wager.

In Chapter One we introduced several Scorecards to illustrate the extraordinary returns that can be earned by consistently winning 5 percent wagers. Think of 5 percent positions as the equivalent of hitting singles in baseball. The goal is to stay in the game and get on base, not hit home runs every time you come to the plate. The Intelligent Bettor knows that significant returns can be earned if he just keeps cranking out single after single. When the Intelligent Bettor steps into the batter's box, he is not only selective about what pitches he swings at, but equally focused on getting his bat on the ball. He is a contact hitter and doesn't go down swinging very often.

The greatest risk to your sports betting capital is the wipeout — losing all or most of your betting capital — and it is caused by two very bad mistakes made by lots of sports bettors. The first is the "sure thing" trap, where the bettor finds a game he thinks will be a "sure thing." Then, because he is convinced it is a sure thing, he exponentially increases the amount of his wager. Instead of sticking with his 5 percent wager, he increases it to 10, 15, or even 20 percent. The second mistake is betting exotic propositions like three- and four-team parlays because they appear to promise extraordinary payouts, even though the odds are stacked highly against him. Such bettors are trying to hit grand slams every time they step up to the plate. They grip the bat hard, grit their teeth and swing away without discipline. They haven't adopted a singles-hitter mentality. They don't know that the bettor who is always trying to hit the ball out of the park strikes out the most. And pretty soon they are out of money.

The Intelligent Bettor knows that wipeouts are a financial disaster. He understands the cruelty of the arithmetic associated with big losses and knows that if he suffers a 50 percent loss on his money, he has to earn 100 percent just to break even! Yes, as all savvy investors know, if you lose half your investment capital, it takes a Herculean effort just to get back to where you started. As a result of this harsh reality, the Intelligent Bettor views his sports betting capital as precious, and he uses proven risk management techniques to protect it.

The Intelligent Bettor doesn't just manage his money by hitting singles. He also guards his capital by shopping for value, like a prudent consumer who clips coupons and is on the lookout for sales. He does comparison pricing and stays within his budget. He places his bets with more than one sports book, so he can put his money down where the prices are best.[19]

5. Discipline: Staying the Course Will Get You to Your Goal

Discipline is the glue that binds everything together in sports betting. Discipline is the trait that leads to consistency. And it is consistent application that allows a well-designed and thought-out system to produce successful results over and over again.

The New England Patriots and Bill Belichick are regarded as having one of the most successful systems in the NFL, and perhaps in all of sports. Every year players come and go, but the Patriots are able to reload and compete for the championship almost every season; a player leaves and they pick up another one that is just right for their system. Their sense of value received for the money paid out is as acute as that of any sports franchise. And so it was when they made the difficult decision to replace Drew Bledsoe with Tom Brady as the quarterback of the team. Bledsoe had been

---

19 Money management principles are discussed in more detail in Chapter Six, and value shopping is reviewed in Chapter Seven.

the face of the franchise for more than a decade, but feeling that his skills were receding, Belichick was confident about calling upon Brady.

As a rookie Brady spent his off-hours as if there were no off-hours. When everyone else was gone for the day, he would go out and practice, using some of the receivers from the practice squad. What he was doing in those extra practices set Brady apart. He was not just telling his receivers, let's run a down and out, or a square in, he was calling plays as if the players were in pressurized game-time situations. He was also unobtrusive in his preparation, as if it were a private thing — always sitting in a small office, burying himself in film and comparing it with the playbook. Possessing the discipline required to drive himself so hard has made Tom Brady a three-time Super Bowl champion and one of the greatest quarterbacks to play in the NFL.

In Chapter One we looked at Scorecard 1.2, which showed how, with beginning capital of $10,000, you could win $80,000 in a year, assuming a 60 percent Win Rate, based on $500 wagers and 20 wagers per week. We saw how the winnings increase astronomically as the Win Rate increases. At a 70 percent Win Rate, your winnings rise to $185,000. That means the two-game difference between winning 14 games a week instead of 12 is worth *$105,000* over the course of a year. And once you have all the other fundamental principles in place — a better model, superior information, risk control and money management — it is *discipline* that determines how much money you will make. Because let's be honest, it takes discipline to make 1,000 high-quality bets in a year, just as it took discipline for Tom Brady to become a great quarterback for the New England Patriots. The Intelligent Investor knows that with discipline, huge financial rewards are within his grasp. The returns for a 60 percent Win Rate are spectacular; at 70 percent they are truly eye-popping. But without discipline, all is lost.

Successful Sports Betting: A Review of the Essentials

The *Get In and Win* System is based on established principles that have been used successfully in the financial markets for years to generate superior profits. Because these elements are essential to your success, it's worth taking a minute to review them:

- ➢ Sports betting presents an opportunity to earn spectacular profits when you have *a better model* that gives you an edge over the other sports bettors.
- ➢ Having *superior information* (not to be confused with more information) will give you the confidence to act on your contrarian instincts.
- ➢ Risk in sports betting can be managed by being highly selective with your bets. Since there are no called strikes in sports wagering, *selectivity is always in your favor.*
- ➢ The first rule of making money is *don't lose money*. Proper money management and sensibly diversifying your bets provides a Margin of Safety and helps minimize losses.
- ➢ Successful sports bettors look at the big picture and plan for winning over the long run, which requires *enormous discipline* and the ability to postpone gratification.

By now you're probably asking, "So how do I make this all work in practice? How do I know what information to use, and where do I even begin?" OK, let's get started.

Searching for Value

"Price is what you pay. Value is what you get."

Warren Buffett

Novice sports bettors often think the way to make money is by simply picking the game winners. While that has an undeniable logic, successful betting is rarely that easy. Unfortunately, just being able to pick winners isn't enough. That's because you have to get over another hurdle to make a successful bet: You must account for the point spread. After taking the point spread into consideration, losing teams can still be a winning bet. Because of that, winning consistently is about identifying value on either side of the point spread, not just picking the game winners. That's where the *Get In and Win* System comes in. *Get In and Win* is a systematic process designed to help you identify which side of the point spread represents the most value. Finding value so that you can make money — no matter who wins the game — is the objective.

Consider an NFL game between the New York Giants and the Pittsburgh Steelers with a point spread that makes the Steelers 3-point favorites (written Pittsburgh -3). If you have read this far, you know that Pittsburgh -3 doesn't mean that the Steelers are a field goal better than the Giants. All it means is that 3 points in favor of the Steelers is required to balance the books and equally divide the amount wagered on the game. The 3-point differential now provides the Intelligent Bettor using the *Get*

In and Win System with the opportunity to find value — and profit — on either side of the point spread.

What do I mean by value? To illustrate, let's jump ahead and say that after applying the *Get In and Win* System to this game, our analysis shows that New York is actually the better team. In fact, our work shows that New York is actually so much better that we would expect the Giants, not the Steelers, to be favored by 7 points. The Intelligent Bettor sees that at Pittsburgh -3 there is a 10-point difference between his own predicted outcome of the game and the point spread. With a touchdown and field goal differential, the Intelligent Bettor confidently places his bet on the Giants.

Often value is not as apparent as it is for the Giants and Steelers game described above. If finding value were so simple, picking upsets would be all that you would need to do to cash winning tickets. It is far more likely that you are going to find that your prediction about the winner of the game will be in agreement with the sports book. The question then becomes, "By how much will they win?"

Recall in Chapter Two that we had another NFL game between Dallas and New England where the point spread was New England -7. Let's say that after applying the *Get In and Win* System to this game, our forecast shows that New England should win, but by only 3 points. The "value" bet in this instance would then be to take Dallas and the 7 points, even though we think New England will win the game. Should the game turn out as we expect, with New England winning by only a field goal, then our bet would also be a winner, even though our pick — Dallas — is the losing team. As this example shows, in point spread wagering it is possible for a team to lose the game and still be a winning bet, because of the boost in points provided by the spread. On the other hand, it is possible for a team to win the game and still be a losing bet because they were unable to overcome the point spread handicap. That is why it is imperative to know which side of the point spread represents the best value.

So how do you assess value? The *Get In and Win* System will teach you exactly how, using a combination of time-tested Wall Street investment principles and winning team management philosophies as practiced by Billy Beane of the Oakland A's. You will learn how to think like the

Intelligent Bettor and find those propositions most likely to make you money.

Value in Investing

As a young stock analyst, I had the good fortune to spend some time as an apprentice to Bob Kahn. Bob was a wise, seasoned investor with more than 50 years of experience on Wall Street. In fact, Bob had spent the earlier part of his career studying under the security analysis master Ben Graham, and working with the legendary investor Warren Buffett. Bob described the practice of investing as the relentless pursuit of value — with value being defined as the difference between the price quote on the stock exchange and its actual worth. Bob always knew the true worth of the stocks he was valuing. If Coca-Cola shares that he had appraised as being worth $65 a share were actually being offered on the stock market at $55, he would buy the stock, with the expectation of realizing a $10 profit per share in the not-too-distant future.

In describing the role of a stock analyst, Bob would tell the story about the Greek philosopher Diogenes. As the fable goes, Diogenes was obsessed with discovering the truth. Diogenes was so passionate in his pursuit of truth that he would carry his lighted lantern through the streets of Athens in broad daylight.

"Any luck, Diogenes?"

Bob would always say that a successful securities analyst needed to pursue the determination of stock value with the same persistence that Diogenes showed in seeking the truth.

While there are many ways to think about value in business and investment, the best investors I know view it this way. Imagine that you and a partner own a business, and every day your partner comes around and names a price at which he will either buy your stake or sell you his. Even though the business may have relatively stable economic characteristics, your partner is an emotional sort, and as a result his prices will be all over the place. When there is only good news affecting the business, he feels euphoric and names a very high price because he fears that you will snap up his stake and rob him of imminent gains. At other times, he is depressed and can see nothing but bad times ahead for the business and the world. On those occasions, he will name a very low price, since he is terrified you will unload your share of the business on him. Your partner's emotions work in your favor because they provide you with the opportunity to profit from the difference between his fluctuating price and the *real* value of the business. Your goal is to sell to your partner when things look great and he is willing to pay more than the actual value. Selling high allows you to profit from your partner's overinflated enthusiasm. Conversely, when things for your business seem at their worst and your partner names a very low price, your goal is to buy his stake and take advantage of his fear.

Great investors recognize when things look better than they really are and sell their overpriced positions at more than their actual value. Selling Internet stocks like Yahoo and AOL in the late '90s when they were over-priced would have been a great way to profit from the greed that was prevalent in the stock market at that time. Conversely, when things seem at their worst, it is usually an opportunity to buy at very low prices. Sir John Templeton, the great value investor, made a fortune for himself in the financial markets by "buying at the point of maximum pessimism."

At the annual meeting for Berkshire Hathaway shareholders in early 2010, Warren Buffet lamented what a terrible year 2009 was for investors, compared to the good times of 2008. Now most people would say that 2008 was a terrible year — the S&P 500 lost 38.5 percent of its value — and 2009 represented a welcome comeback for stocks. But from Buffett's perspective, 2008 yielded fantastic buying opportunities because stocks had become so cheap. By 2009, the bargains were picked over and the hot deals were gone. Average investors, ruled by fear in bad times and greed in good times, mistakenly sell stocks when they are low and buy them when they are high. Buffett does the opposite, a strategy that has made him (at this writing) the third-richest man in the world.

In the same way, a contrarian attitude in sports betting will make you richer. The same fear and greed that cause stock investors to buy high and sell low cause mispricings in the sports betting market and present value-oriented bettors with great opportunities.

Billy Beane and Value

In Michael Lewis' book *Moneyball*, Oakland A's general manager Billy Beane explains how he employs the concepts of value and mispricing to his benefit in putting together a winning baseball team. Beane's problem, in a nutshell, was that he had $40 million to spend on 25 baseball players. His opponents — much richer teams in big media markets — had already spent $126 million on their own 25 players, and held perhaps another $100 million in reserve. What do you do with your $40 million to avoid humiliating defeat? "What you don't do," says Beane in the book, "is what the Yankees do. If we do what the Yankees do, we lose every time, because they are doing it with three times more money than we are."

Beane believed that the market for baseball players was so mispriced and the general concept of sound baseball strategy so misunderstood that there was a great opportunity for sophisticated management, using a systematic approach, to "run circles around taller piles of cash." He began the process by exploring it as if it were a math problem. He looked at the places where traditional baseball stats didn't tell the whole truth or, as Beane would say, "lie" about the situation. His goal was to analyze and value the events that occur on a baseball field differently and more accurately than they had ever been assessed before.

For example, one player who caught Beane's eye in 2000 was an overweight, nerdy-looking Jewish kid from Cincinnati. In college, Kevin Youkilis looked nothing like a major league baseball star. His dainty plate stance — he held the bat high above his shoulders, cradling it between his thumb and forefinger as if it were a teacup — made it look like he'd rather be doing anything other than swinging at fastballs. And in fact, he didn't swing very often, drawing more walks than anyone Beane could remember. As a result, he quietly got on base a lot — and then went on to score runs. But because he wasn't a home-run hitter, Beane's own scouts ignored Youkilis. That year, the Red Sox picked him up cheap as an eighth-round draft choice. Beane tried but failed to get the Sox to trade Youkilis, who of course went on to be an All-Star player (he lost weight and developed into quite a fine hitter and fielder as well as a walker) with (at this writing) two World Series rings. But in 2000, according to the conventional wisdom, Youkilis was a nobody. Even though Beane was not able to get Youkilis on the A's roster, he could see Youkilis' ultimate value on the baseball diamond long before it was apparent to most everyone else.

And it was Beane's keen system for valuing talent that made him successful, turning the A's into one of baseball's winningest teams as measured by seasonal win-loss records and playoff berths. Using arithmetic, sound baseball knowledge and good judgment, Beane developed his own unique method for appraising the value of baseball players. Applying his system in a disciplined way enabled him to transform one of the poorest (financially speaking) teams in baseball into one that contends for a championship almost every year. As a rival general manager once said (raising one hand as high as he could and lowering the other to his knees), "Billy is up here and everyone else is down here." There is no question that Billy Beane has become one of the best in his game.

Diogenes, Billy Beane and the Intelligent Bettor

Because sports betting is an exercise in finding value, or "the truth" about the outcome of a game, the Intelligent Bettor thinks in a value-seeking way. The Intelligent Bettor approaches a wager just the way successful investors think about buying or selling a stake in a business, or profiting from the fear and greed in the investment markets. The Intelligent Bettor looks for pricing inefficiencies in the posted line in the same manner that Billy Beane evaluates baseball talent and Warren Buffett values potential investments. Like Diogenes, you must be single-minded and relentless in seeking the truth about the point spread so you can make winning bets and put cash in your pocket.

The Gold Is in the Numbers

To find value, you need to have an edge over the other sports bettors. That advantage comes from looking at sports from a different perspective, using statistics that others do not pay attention to or know how to interpret properly for profit. As the psychologist Carl Jung said, "The gold is in the dark." It is in the dark places where others cannot see that you, as the

Intelligent Bettor using the *Get In and Win* methods as your lantern, will find the information and value you are seeking so the treasure can be yours.

Break Through the Box Score

Consider the traditional basketball box score. Like most people, I can't watch as many games as I would like, so I keep up with how teams and players are doing by looking at the box scores in the newspaper or, these days, by scanning a variety of sports-related websites. But the box score is limited because its purpose is to summarize what happened during the game — not *how* or *why* it happened. While the box score does provide some useful information, the story it presents is incomplete. It is the Cliffs Notes version of the game, providing a general overview but leaving out a lot of the important information that you need to know to win your bets.

Table 4.1 presents the box score from the 2011 NCAA Tournament Final Four Game played between Kentucky and Connecticut.

Table 4.1   Kentucky vs. Connecticut Box Score

Final	1	2	T
KENTY	21	34	55
UCONN	31	25	56

KENTUCKY WILDCATS												
Player	MIN	FGM-A	3GM-A	FTM-A	OFF	DEF	TOT	A	PF	STL	TO	BLK	PTS
Josh Harrellson	28:00	3-6	0-0	0-1	3	1	4	2	3	2	0	0	6
Brandon Knight	40:00	6-23	3-11	2-2	2	6	8	5	1	2	3	0	17
Terrence Jones	38:00	5-8	1-2	0-5	4	11	15	1	1	4	2	1	11
Darius Miller	26:00	1-7	1-4	1-2	1	2	3	2	2	1	2	0	4
DeAndre Liggins	34:00	1-7	1-5	1-2	0	0	0	2	4	2	1	2	4
Doron Lamb	27:00	5-10	3-5	0-0	0	0	0	0	1	0	2	0	13
Elroy Vargas	7:00	0-1	0-0	0-0	3	2	5	0	0	0	0	0	0
Total	200	21-62	9-27	4-12	13	22	35	12	12	11	10	3	55
		33.9%	33.3%	33.3%	Team Rebs: 2					Total TO: 10		

CONNECTICUT HUSKIES												
Player	MIN	HFM-A	3GM-A	FTM-A	OFF	DEF	TOT	A	PF	STL	TO	BLK	PTS
Jeremy Lamb	38:00	5-8	0-2	2-2	1	8	9	4	1	0	2	0	12
Kemba Walker	40:00	6-15	1-5	5-6	1	5	6	7	1	2	4	1	18
Alex Oriakhi	27:00	4-6	0-0	0-0	2	8	10	1	2	0	1	1	8
Tyler Olander	5:00	1-1	0-0	0-0	0	1	1	0	0	0	1	0	2
Roscoe Smith	29:00	3-6	0-0	0-0	1	7	8	0	2	0	1	0	6
Niels Giffey	8:00	0-0	0-0	0-0	1	0	1	0	1	1	1	0	0
Charles Okwandu	16:00	2-3	0-0	0-0	0	1	1	0	2	2	2	1	4
Shabazz Napier	27:00	1-7	0-4	2-2	0	2	2	4	3	0	3	0	4
Jamal Coombs-McDaniel	9:00	1-3	0-1	0-1	0	0	0	0	1	0	0	0	2
Donnell Beverly	1:00	0-0	0-0	0-0	0	0	0	0	0	0	0	0	0
Total	200	23-49	1-12	9-11	6	32	38	16	13	5	15	3	56
		46.9%	8.3%	81.8%	Team Rebs: 0					Total TO: 15		

GAME INFO

Date: Saturday, April 2, 2011 8:49PM
Location: Reliant Stadium, Houston, Texas
Officials: John Higgings, Les Jones, Mark Whitehead
Attendance: 75421

From the box score, we can tell that it was a low-scoring game, with Connecticut winning 56-55 (major college basketball teams average approximately 71 points per game). The box score also presents a lot of detailed information about each player, such as shots attempted, shots made, minutes played, rebounds, free throws attempted, free throws made and points scored. If you are the everyday fan or a fantasy sports player, this information is fun to know and can even be useful to you. But the Intelligent Bettor requires more, and he knows how to dig deeper to gain better insight.

In any sport, efficiency is the single most important factor that controls winning and losing, and by how much. And as a sports bettor, that is all that matters to you — determining who will win the game and by how much. In football, efficiency can be measured in terms of points per play. In baseball, it is about scoring as many runs as possible before making 27 outs. And in basketball, it comes down to scoring as many points as possible with each possession of the basketball. The traditional basketball box score doesn't tell us much about efficiency, but it does provide the elements to calculate it for those who know where to look and what tools to use.

In the *Get In and Win* NCAA Basketball and NBA Playbooks, you will learn how to analyze basketball box scores in great detail, but let's jump ahead and do a quick *Get In and Win* review of the game played between Connecticut and Kentucky. From the box score, we can see that Connecticut scored 56 points and Kentucky scored 55 points, but we still don't know anything about possessions or efficiency. Upon closer examination, using some other statistics also found in the box score, we can determine the game tempo by calculating the number of possessions for each team— Connecticut and Kentucky each had 63 possessions.[20] A review of each team's prior game history for the season reveals that Connecticut and Kentucky averaged approximately 65 possessions per game and both had a high offensive efficiency ratio (meaning during the regular season both teams excelled at converting scoring opportunities into points). Therefore, since the game was a low-scoring affair with the tempo played at each team's usual pace, we can conclude that offensive efficiency was lower than normal for both teams.

Once we know the number of possessions, we can quickly determine two other important facts about the game: (1) the number of additional scoring opportunities each team was able to generate by rebounding its own misses (getting offensive rebounds) and taking better care of the basketball (minimizing turnovers); and (2) the way each team used its scoring opportunities. Table 4.2 summarizes the game in a much different way than the box score:

---

20 To determine the number of possessions for each team in a basketball game, use this equation: Possessions = Field Goals Attempted - Offensive Rebounds + Turnovers + (0.475 x Free Throws Attempted).

85

Table 4.2

NCAA Tournament
April 2, 2011

	KENTUCKY		CONNECTICUT	
Possessions/Tempo	63		63	
Offensive Rebounds	13		6	
Turnovers	10		15	
Scoring Opportunities Available	66		54	

Scoring Opportunities	Percent successful	Number used	Number of points	Percent successful	Number used	Number of points
3 Point Attempts	27	27		12	12	
3 Point Made	9 33%		27	1 8%		3
2 Point Attempts	35	35		37	37	
2 Point Made	12 34%		24	22 59%		44
Free Throw Attempts ?	12	4		11	5	
Free Throws Made	4 33%		4	9 82%		9
Scoring Opportunities Used		66			54	
Total Number of Points			55			56

Looking at the game from the perspective of possessions and scoring opportunities allows us to see what actually happened during the game and evaluate each team's scoring efficiency. While Connecticut won the game, Kentucky had more scoring opportunities — 66 for Kentucky versus 54 for Connecticut — because Kentucky had more offensive rebounds and fewer turnovers. Despite substantially fewer scoring chances, Connecticut was able to win because they were more *efficient* at converting scoring opportunities into points, especially from the free throw line. With this information in hand, we now know not only that Connecticut won the game but also *why* and *how* they were able to win. Moreover, we have a better basis for predicting how these teams will perform in future games.

There are no future games for these teams!

Legendary coach Frank McGuire at both the University of North Carolina and the University of South Carolina was actually the first to introduce the concept of possessions as a way to analyze performance in basketball. It initially appeared in his book for coaches called *Defensive Basketball*, published in 1966. Dean Smith, a coaching icon at North Carolina, was McGuire's assistant at the time, and he popularized the idea within college basketball coaching circles during his prestigious career. Currently, most NBA teams use some version of possession scoring as a way to evaluate player and team performance. In fact, Dallas Mavericks owner Mark Cuban employs a small army of statisticians to track and evaluate all types of possession-based statistics. Cuban is also the lead investor in Synergy Sports, an Internet-based business that plans to make much of this information available to sports fans for a fee.

Using these same measures of basketball efficiency to make accurate game forecasts, the Intelligent Bettor is able to break through the box score and look at the game in a different way from the average fan. While it is obvious that a team that makes a lot of shots, controls the offensive glass, minimizes turnovers, and gets to the free throw line is going to be very efficient, it gets really interesting when attempting to predict how teams will play against each other. When two strong-rebounding teams that both shoot the ball well square off, it is likely that turnovers will decide the game, because the team that has fewer turnovers will have more scoring opportunities unless the other team is more efficient (as was the case when Connecticut defeated Kentucky). The winner of a basketball game is simply the team that maximizes the points scored when they possess the ball, and limits the points scored when its opponent has the ball. Thinking about basketball in terms of possessions, scoring opportunities and efficiency will give you an advantage over the average sports bettor, who is still looking at the box score in the traditional way as his source for wagering inspiration.

Probability x Payoff = Team Value

Just as with investing, it is in the numbers that you will find gold in sports betting. Analyzing numbers involves math. Now, before you begin groaning about how you hated high school algebra, let me assure you that the *Get In and Win* System requires nothing more than addition, subtraction and multiplication. That's it!

On the other hand, those who like numbers will find the math in this section interesting, and closely related to expected-value calculations used in finance. Understanding the math will help you develop a keener insight into sports betting, especially when money-line wagering is discussed in Chapter Nine. But for those who are less interested in the computations, don't worry: All the formulas discussed here are presented later in easy-to-use Score Sheets and charts. Those worksheets provide all the information you need to be an Intelligent Bettor and make accurate, reliable assessments of value.

Forget for a moment everything you know (or think you know) about sports betting and just focus for a moment on this equation:

$$\text{Probability x Payoff} = \text{Team Value}$$

In the equation, *probability* means the likelihood of each team's winning the game, expressed as a percentage. *Payoff* represents the dollar amount you will collect if you win the wager — the amount wagered plus the profits. The *team value* tells you how much you would wager on a team given two things: (1) the probability you have assigned to the team of winning the game; and (2) the potential payoff for winning the wager.

Let's assume we have a game between Team A and Team B. Based on the *Get In and Win* principles that you will learn later, you have concluded that Team A has a 70 percent likelihood of beating Team B, and you are willing to enter into a standard point spread bet that pays out $100 for every $110 put at risk. For now, we will assume that all we have to do is pick the winner and not pick against the point spread. Using the team value equation, we get the following team value for Team A:

$$70\% \times \$210 = \$147$$

Conversely, the team value for Team B is calculated as follows:

$$30\% \times \$210 = \$63$$

In this simple example, the equation tells us that at an assumed probability of winning the game of 70 percent, we would be willing to wager $147 (or less) for the opportunity to collect $210 if Team A wins the game. At the same time, the equation tells us that we would be willing to wager $63 (or less) for the opportunity to collect $210 if Team B wins the game.

Note that both teams represent potential value. The equation simply tells us the maximum price we would be willing to pay to place a wager on each team. Unfortunately, sports betting is not so easy that we can simply perform a team value computation on every game and then name the price at which we would be willing to set our wager. In the real world, we also need to adjust for the point spread.

So let's return now to the example that we introduced at the beginning of Chapter Two, where we had New England -7 versus Dallas. We believe that New England will win the game because New England is better than Dallas. Let's say that without the point spread, we think that New England has a 65 percent probability of winning the game, and Dallas has a 35 percent likelihood of winning.[21] But *with* the point spread, we think that New England has only a 45 percent chance of both winning and covering the 7-point handicap. That leaves Dallas with a 55 percent likelihood of losing by less than 7 points or winning outright.

Using the team value equation, we write the following:

New England Team Value
45% x $210 = $94.50

Dallas Team Value
55% x $210 = $115.50

Since the outlay required to bet is $110, we would place our bet on Dallas, even though we expect New England to win the game. The team value, or expected payout from wagering on Dallas, of $115.50 is greater than the $110 price of making the wager. That's a good deal!

---

21 In Chapter Nine, you will learn how to convert the point spread and the money line into expected winning percentages for each team.

By contrast, the team value or expected payout from a wager on New England is less than the $110 asking price. That means even though New England is the game's favorite, a bet on New England (under the given point spread) is a losing proposition. That's the polite term. Some would call it a sucker's bet.

The point of this exercise is to show that even a team with a relatively high likelihood of winning can be either a very good or a very bad bet, and the difference between the two is determined by only one thing — the point spread. The point spread is the dividing line between paying too much to bet and finding a bargain. This basic principle is the most important thing I can tell you about sports betting. Fortunately, the vast majority of your competitors don't get it.

You Pay a High Price for a Cheery Consensus

It's the same in the stock market, where the *price paid* sets the dividing line between a good investment and a bad one. Contrary to common knowledge, an excellent company can be a bad investment and a bad company can be a good investment. That's because investors often have unrealistic expectations for excellent companies and bid up their prices to excessive levels, while bad companies are underappreciated and their stock can be purchased at favorable prices.

As an example, consider Microsoft's and Apple's businesses a decade ago and the returns that an investor would have earned from owning each company's stock between then and now. Ten years ago, Microsoft's Office suite of software products and its Windows operating system dominated the personal and business computing markets, with earnings accelerating as far as analysts could project. On the other hand, Apple (before the iPod, iPhone and iPad) was a much smaller company with slowing sales that produced software and hardware products primarily for the academic market; many professional investors questioned its long-term viability as a stand-alone enterprise. On September 28, 2001, Microsoft's stock was priced at approximately $25 per share (after considering stock splits) and traded at an extraordinarily high price/earnings ratio (44 times record earnings).[22] Apple's stock was priced at approximately $8 per share (after considering stock splits) and traded at a much more reasonable price/earnings ratio, especially considering Apple's poor earnings in 2001.

Let's fast-forward to 2011 and look at the two companies' financial performance over a 10-year period. On September 28, 2011, Microsoft's stock traded at the same price ($25) that it did on September 28, 2001. That's right, investors holding Microsoft shares from September 28, 2001, to September 28, 2011, made no money. Incredible! And it's even more amazing considering that Microsoft's earnings per share increased almost five times during that period (from $.57 per share to $2.69 per share). That means that despite maintaining a dominant position in the computer market and increasing its earnings by almost five times, owners of Microsoft's stock had no gain to show for sticking with their investment in the company for 10 years. What happened? It's simple: In 2001, the price for Microsoft stock was way too high based on what turned out to be its future potential financial performance. Even though its financial performance was very good, it wasn't good enough to overcome an extremely high price/earnings ratio handicap of 44 times earnings.

Now consider Apple's financial performance during that same period. Apple's share price rose from $8 in September 2001 to an astonishing $397 by September 28, 2011, providing extraordinary returns to its stock investors. Beginning with the October 2001 rollout of the original iPod (which completely transformed the music industry), Apple introduced innovative product after product; earnings grew from $.31 per share in September 2001 to $25.26 per share in September 2011. Investors who had done their homework and correctly assessed the potential for the iPod were rewarded with huge investment profits following the well-known Wall Street axiom "Buy low and sell high."

When it comes to sports betting, imagine the New Orleans Saints as Microsoft and the Detroit Lions as Apple for the 2010-11 NFL season.

---

22 The average price/earnings ratio on the U.S. stock market since the 1870s has been about 15. A price/earnings ratio for a stock is similar to the point spread assigned to the favorite in a game: the larger the price/earnings ratio (or the point spread) the more difficult it is to make money on a stock (or for a favorite to "cover" the point spread).

The Saints entered the 2010-11 season as the defending Super Bowl Champions, having logged a record of 13-3 the previous regular season. At the other end of the spectrum, the Lions were coming off a 2009-10 season where they had won just two games and finished in the basement of the NFC North. Just like Microsoft in 2001, it appeared that New Orleans had everything going its way for 2010-11, and consequently all the sports betting public could see was green grass, white lines and touchdowns in the Saints' future. For Detroit, 2010-11 looked like another season of interceptions, fumbles and dropped passes. But like Apple, Detroit was about to go through a transformation led by two young skilled players: quarterback Matthew Stafford and receiver Calvin Johnson. And sure enough, while New Orleans finished the 2010-11 with a regular season record of 11-5 and qualified for the playoffs, the Saints posted a losing record of 7-9 against the point spread, leaving bettors who had consistently picked them to cover the point spread disappointed (just like Microsoft investors). On the other hand, the transformed Lions improved to 6-10 during the 2010-11 regular season, but did even more for sports bettors who had correctly anticipated their improvement by rewarding them with a 12-4 record against the point spread.

It's All About Value

Consider what all this means for finding value and making profitable wagers. To be an Intelligent Bettor, you must determine which team offers the best value at the price offered as represented by the point spread. The Intelligent Bettor only wants to know which wagers have a positive expected return and which do not. He is in search of those teams with team values that exceed the price of placing the bet. Using this approach, everything but *value* fades from view.

Do you really think that most sports bettors think this way? Of course not! They find teams they like, and hope for the best price. They find the winner and then bet. They figure if they know their teams, the winning will take care of itself. They believe if they only study the past performances long enough, the winner will jump off the page.

But the Intelligent Bettor knows there is no such thing as liking a team. The only thing that matters is identifying an attractive mispricing between the point spread and the actual value. He has a clear understanding of what the price for each game should be, and he is prepared to seize the opportunities based on the line posted.

Margin of Safety

We have seen how the concept of value shifts with the point spread. From that observation, it is easy to see that value is a relative term — some games present better wagering values than others. When a game presents an extremely good value — typically because the betting line posted by the sports book is substantially different than the line you have calculated — professional investors, like me, call that a *Margin of Safety*.

The Margin of Safety is the core concept around which all valuation principles in the *Get In and Win* System revolve. Placing a bet with a Margin of Safety is like getting a "discount" — a discount to what the point spread actually is on a game, as opposed to what you have forecast it to be. It is similar to waiting for something to go on sale before you buy it. In the financial markets it is like buying a share of Coca-Cola for $55 when you know it is really worth $65. The Margin of Safety is the difference between the point spread and the actual value of the game.

Using the examples at the beginning of this chapter, the Margin of Safety for the football game between the Pittsburgh Steelers and the New York Giants game is 10 points — calculated as the difference between the posted line of the Steelers -3 and our forecast for the game, which would have been Giants -7. This means that our analysis of the outcome of the game could be off by almost a touchdown and a field goal without the danger of taking a loss. For the game between the Dallas Cowboys and the New England Patriots, the Margin of Safety would be 4 points, which is the difference between the sports book's point spread of Patriots -7 and our forecasted point spread of the Patriots -3. Placing a wager when there is a Margin of Safety provides strong protection against losing money.

The concept of the Margin of Safety goes back to the philosophy that minimizing losses is every bit as important as placing winning wagers. Why do bargains exist for sports bettors? Remember, the point spread is devised by the sports book to guarantee that the amount bet on any particular game is equally divided between the two teams. It is not a prediction of its outcome, which is not the sports book's concern. Making an accurate assessment of the most likely outcome of the game is a job for you, the Intelligent Bettor. And the Intelligent Better knows that there are plenty of wagering opportunities out there at a substantial discount, if he only takes the time to do the research, and employs the discipline and patience to be selective.

The Intelligent Bettor insists on a significant Margin of Safety before putting his precious betting capital on the line. After performing a thorough analysis using the *Get In and Win* System, he will come up with his own line for the game — a line that he believes represents good wagering value. If his calculation of the outcome of a game is only slightly different than the point spread posted, he is not interested in betting on that game. While determining an accurate forecast for the outcome of a game is what the *Get In and Win* System is all about, there will be times when the forecast will be wrong. There is always the chance of the impossible play — a blocked field goal that is returned for a touchdown, a basketball team shooting 70 percent from behind the 3-point line, or a baseball team scoring the walk-off run on a wild pitch. Sports fans live for such moments, of course, and even though they are rare, we all know they can happen. That's why a bettor must have a Margin of Safety — a cushion that absorbs the unexpected game-changers that make sports so exciting.

The larger the Margin of Safety, the better the wagering opportunity, because the chance of losing money decreases. Betting only when there is a significant Margin of Safety puts your wager in a position to withstand adverse developments or lucky plays. When wagers are made on a bargain basis, an unusual play that was not anticipated in your analysis of the game will not necessarily prevent you from winning. The Margin of Safety will then have served its intended purpose.

We will talk more about using actual Margin of Safety calculations to tell you when to bet and when to pass in the next chapter. For now, you should know that the Margin of Safety is the way value is measured. The higher the Margin of Safety (the larger the difference between your forecasted outcome of the game and the point spread), the more value there is. Conversely, the lower the margin of safety (the smaller the difference between your predicted outcome and the sports book's posted line), the less value there is. An acceptable Margin of Safety exists when the betting line you have calculated is substantially different than the one posted by the sports book. In those instances where a significant Margin of Safety exists, it's like getting a dollar bill for 50 cents. What a deal!

A Playbook for Finding Value

"Hope is not a strategy."

Billy Beane, Oakland Athletics General Manager

Get your pencils sharpened and ready — it's time to get down to it. In this chapter, I will show you how to calculate the *value* of each game using *Get In and Win* and taking into account the point spread offered by the sports book and your own analysis of the teams. You will learn a fundamentally sound process for calculating your own custom point spread in a systematic, objective way that is based on the same methods securities analysts use when appraising stocks. To be an Intelligent Bettor, the starting point is coming up with your own point spread so you can compare your forecast to the one posted by the sports book. The difference between your calculated number and the sports book's is referred to in stock market terms as a *mispricing*. And it is where you discover big mispricings (between what your calculations show a game is worth and the quoted price) that you want to place your bet.

To achieve long-term success in sports betting (as well as investing), it is not enough to learn and mechanically apply a few mathematical rules, formulas or statistical models. In sports betting (and in investing), there are way too many variables to consider, and they change far too quickly for such an approach to succeed. Any eighth-grade algebra student can memorize a few basic principles and appear superficially competent, but without real knowledge, disaster awaits. Instead, to succeed consistently, it is necessary to gain a true understanding of the rationale behind the *Get In and Win* models and calculations in order to appreciate how they work so you can apply them properly and use your own special insights to place winning wagers.

The key is not to get sidetracked in your search for value. Stay focused and remember that nothing else matters when you are betting on sports but making an accurate prediction of what the point differential between the two teams will be.[23] Thus, you should only pay attention to statistics and information that are relevant to your forecasting process. It might be interesting to talk about whether Tom Brady is a better quarterback than Aaron Rogers, but that has very little to do with winning sports bets. Because there are lots of games to analyze and your time is limited, you need to work quickly and accurately. The *Get In and Win* System will show you how to focus on what matters so you can push the distractions to the side and make the best use of your time.

The best analysts on Wall Street combine two different approaches to find profitable investments. They start with what is called a "top-down" view, in which they take a comprehensive look at the overall economy and the factors that have a high probability of influencing the economic environment going forward (labor costs, productivity inputs, factory utilization, inventories, etc.). This information is then used to rank the industries that will likely do well based on their economic forecast and to target the top companies in the best industries as potential investments.

After selectively compiling a list of the industries and the companies that have the highest return profiles, they dig deeper into the operations of each selected company from a "bottom-up" perspective, focusing their attention on the specific items that drive corporate performance (such as sales, profit margins and overhead structures). When they hit upon a situation where their top-down view aligns with their bottom-up evaluation, they know have spotted a moneymaking opportunity.

---

23 The specialty wagers such as money lines, totals and propositions are reviewed in detail in Chapter Nine.

Following a similar "top-down" and "bottom-up" process can also benefit sports bettors in their pursuit of profits. The *Get In and Win* System incorporates two original and proprietary methods for your use when calculating your own forecasted point spread: the Value Rating and the Score Sheet. The Value Rating uses a top-down approach that assigns a relative value to each team and then ranks each team on a predetermined scale. The Score Sheet is a bottom-up analysis of the factors influencing the actual performance of each specific team. The power of these methods is in their ease of use. Even though of each of the methods is based on some very sophisticated mathematics, the *Get In and Win* System has simplified their application so that anyone can use them.

Separate *Get In and Win* Playbooks accompany and supplement this book. The Playbooks explain in great detail how to use and maintain the Value Ratings and Score Sheets for each of the major sports: the NFL; college football; the NBA; NCAA basketball; and Major League Baseball. This chapter provides an overview of the methods described in the NFL and NBA Playbooks so that you can become familiar with the concepts supporting the methods and learn how to apply them before moving on to the detailed number crunching covered in the Playbooks.

Value Ratings: The Perfect Predictor

In a perfect world, a sports better is seeking one measurement that will tell him which team will win and which will lose, and by how much — one metric that is easy to understand, accurate and complete. The innovative *Get In and Win* Value Rating is that number. It is the one statistic you have been searching for. Carefully constructed and properly maintained, it can be a complete measure of a team's most likely actual performance. The *Get In and Win* Value Rating should be the cornerstone of your handicapping process; when applied properly, it will lead to great financial reward. This single number representing a team's overall strength can tell your more at a glance than reading multiple newspapers or spending countless hours combing the Internet, sifting through information that is of little or no value.

The benefit of using *Get In and Win*'s Value Ratings as the core of your analysis is that they are objective arbiters of value. Value Ratings are dispassionate, easy to understand and complete. When you use Value Ratings, the piles of individual and team statistics that bog down your game analysis suddenly disappear. Proper Value Ratings combined with your own knowledge and judgment are extremely accurate predictors of the outcomes of games. And as an added benefit, Value Ratings are an efficient way to correctly analyze a number of games in a short period of time.

The *Get In and Win* Value Ratings are an improvement over the familiar power rankings that can be found on every popular Internet website focused on sports (ESPN.com, SportingNews.com, FoxSports.com, CBSSports.com, etc.). By way of background, sports fans have been using traditional power rankings for years as a way to rate where teams stand in terms of strength and skill in relation to their opponents. Although the *Get In and Win* Value Ratings and traditional power rankings are both relative value measures that share a primary purpose — comparing one team to another — there are some very distinct differences.

To begin with, most traditional power ratings have a similar underlying methodology and therefore suffer from the same fatal flaw. Numerical values are assigned to certain statistics, and then all the data is rolled up into one final power ranking number, without regard to whether or not there is a valid basis for combining the factors. For example, one popular power ranking system for football mixes together the following inputs:

> Rush-to-Pass Ratio + Total Play Differential + Expected Yards Per Rush + Expected Yards Per Pass Attempt + Total Yardage Differential + Turnover Differential + Yards Per Point + Plays Per First Down + Momentum + Last Game Between the Teams + Home Field Advantage = Power Rating

Wow, that's a lot of data! And given the complexity, it's hard to know whether or not it is accurate, but it certainly isn't simple or efficient to use. Moreover, it incorporates many statistics that don't matter to a sports bettor, whose only interest is making an accurate prediction about the point differential between two teams in a game. That's why sports bettors need something better than traditional power rankings to perform their wagering analysis.

Created just for sports betting, *Get In and Win*'s own unique Value Rating is the next logical progression in terms of sophistication and simplicity.[24] The Value Rating framework is based on my extensive research showing that team strength from top to bottom in all major sports can be quantified and remains constant from year to year. It is only the individual teams themselves that move around within the ranking system. The numerical rating for the best team, the second-best team, the third-best team and so on remains the same from year to year. The exercise then becomes determining which team is the best and which is the worst, and in what order the other teams fall in between.

Consider the NFL and its 32 teams. Let's assume that after considerable mathematical modeling we know that the best team in the league always plays to a Value Rating of 113 and the worst team always plays to a Value Rating of 87. The Value Rating for an average team is 100. This means that year in and year out (on a relative value basis) the best team in the NFL is approximately 26 points (113 - 87) better than the worst team. And the difference between the best team and an average team is 13 points (113 - 100). This same general Value Rating methodology holds true for the relationship between each of the other 30 teams in the NFL, meaning that there are 32 fixed positions on the Value Ratings scale for the NFL and it is only the teams that move around within those values from year to year and throughout the season. The Value Rating scale itself does not change.

---

24 To determine the validity of new investment models, investment professionals often use a technique called backtesting, which involves determining how reliably a new algorithm will likely perform using past data and Monte Carlo simulations. The *Get In and Win* Value Rating models are based on the extensively backtested work published by statisticians Jeff Sagarin and Kenneth Massey and verified by me. Sagarin provides ratings on sports teams to *USA Today* (since 1985), the NCAA basketball tournament selection committee (since 1984) and the Bowl Championship Series (since 1998). Kenneth Massey is a professor of mathematics at Carson-Newman College, and his college football team ratings have been a component of the Bowl Championship Series selection process since 1999.

For example, for the 2008-09 NFL season, the Pittsburgh Steelers were the top-rated team by the end of the season. Pittsburgh started the season at moderately above average and moved to the top of the list. At the other end of the spectrum, the Detroit Lions ended up being the worst team in the NFL at the end of that same season. Like the Steelers, Detroit started the season in the middle of the pack, but the Lions went the other direction, working their way to the bottom. The prior season, the New England Patriots were rated the best in the league and the St. Louis Rams were the worst. Using the *Get In and Win* Value Rating method, Pittsburgh and New England each had the highest ranking of 113 at the end of the season, when they were the highest-rated teams, and Detroit and St. Louis each had the lowest rating of 87 at the end of the season, when they were at the bottom.

Since the Value Rating framework for the NFL remains consistent from year to year, and because the Value Rating for each of the 32 positions within the framework has already been assigned,[25] your job is to determine the appropriate place on the rating scale for each team — and properly adjust each team's position throughout the season to reflect the changes in the way teams are playing. The Value Rating approach is dynamic, recognizing that teams play at different levels throughout the year. Once you have established your Value Ratings,[26] they require some, but not a lot, of effort to maintain. Keep reading and you will learn how to apply NFL and

---

25 You will note that some of the positions have the same Value Rating. For example, the Value Rating for positions 4 and 5 is 108 and the Value Rating for positions 21, 22 and 23 is 96. So don't spend a lot of time determining if a team should be ranked 4 or 5, because in terms of betting value there is no difference — they are the same.

26 To establish the initial top-to-bottom ranking of the teams on the *Get In and Win* Value Rating scale, consider referencing Ken Massey's ratings (www.masseyratings.com) and Jeff Sagarin's ratings (www.sagarin.com) to help you make your own determination about the appropriate order — not the specific team values, because in the *Get In and Win* System team values are assigned based on a team's position on the Value Rating scale. Remember, it is the team's movement up or down the Value Rating scale that causes team values to adjust; the numerical value assigned to each position on the Value Rating scale itself does not change.

NBA Value Ratings, and update them using a combination of processes that were initially developed by Bob Succi, the legendary sports book manager at the Stardust Casino; Joe Del Popolo, the founder of *GamePlan* magazine; Phil Steele, publisher of the widely read Phil Steele college and professional football annuals; and Mike Lee, a well-known professional sports bettor.

Value Ratings Applied, Using the NFL as an Example

A simplified version of the *Get In and Win* Value Rating process and how it applies to the NFL is presented here as an example.

For Week Seven of the 2008-09 NFL season, the Value Ratings are reported in Table 5.1:

Table 5.1

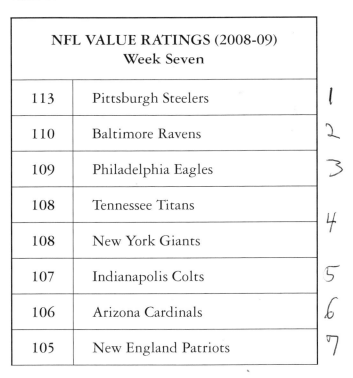

NFL VALUE RATINGS (2008-09) Week Seven	
113	Pittsburgh Steelers
110	Baltimore Ravens
109	Philadelphia Eagles
108	Tennessee Titans
108	New York Giants
107	Indianapolis Colts
106	Arizona Cardinals
105	New England Patriots

103	Carolina Panthers	8
102	Atlanta Falcons	9
102	Dallas Cowboys	
101	San Diego Chargers	10
101	Minnesota Vikings	
100	Chicago Bears	11
99	Tampa Bay Buccaneers	
99	Miami Dolphins	12
98	New Orleans Saints	13
98	Houston Texans	
97	New York Jets	14
97	Washington Redskins	
96	Green Bay Packers	
96	San Francisco 49ers	15
96	Denver Broncos	
95	Jacksonville Jaguars	16
95	Buffalo Bills	
94	Cincinnati Bengals	17
94	Cleveland Browns	

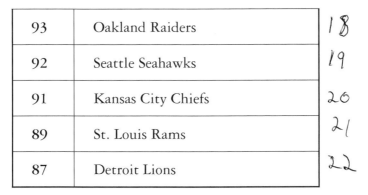

93	Oakland Raiders	18
92	Seattle Seahawks	19
91	Kansas City Chiefs	20
89	St. Louis Rams	21
87	Detroit Lions	22

To make predictions for upcoming games, simply compare the ratings of the teams playing in the game and add three more points to the home team's Value Rating to reflect the statistically significant home field advantage. For example, a home team with a Value Rating of 103 (the Carolina Panthers in Table 5.1) would be favored by 5 points over a visiting team having a Value Rating of 101 (the Minnesota Vikings in Table 5.1). By the same token, a visiting team with a Value Rating of 108 (the Tennessee Titans in Table 5.1) would be favored by 6 points when playing against a home team having a Value Rating of 99 (the Tampa Bay Buccaneers in Table 5.1).

More specifically, in Week Seven of the 2008-2009 NFL season, the New England Patriots played the Denver Broncos in Massachusetts. The point spread posted by most of the sports books for the game was:

```
Denver
New England     -3
```

Using the NFL Value Ratings above, New England was rated at 105 and Denver was rated at 96. New England was the home team, so 3 points are added to New England's rating, making their at-home Value Rating 108. Using the Value Ratings to determine the predicted outcome of the game, you would simply subtract 108 from 96. Let's do the math: 108 minus 96 equals 12. Therefore, you would expect New England to win the game by 12 points. It's that easy — determine the appropriate ranking for each team within the Value Rating method, adjust for home field advantage, and then compare the Value Rating for each of the teams playing in a game. Presto, you have your own forecasted point spread for the outcome of the game.

Next you compare your Value Rating forecast of the point spread to the sports book's posted point spread to determine if there is a substantial difference between your forecast and the point spread. In this example, the sports book's posted line says the Patriots are favored by 3 points. But your Value Rating forecast predicts that New England will win by 12 points. That means there is a whopping 9-point difference between the sports book's posted point spread and the Value Rating prediction, so a bet on New England is certainly a high-value bet. And in this instance, a wager on New England would have also been a winning bet, because the Patriots actually beat the Broncos 41-7.

Updating NFL Value Ratings

To update your value ratings, simply compare the final score of the game to your projected point spread and adjust the Value Rating for each team according to Table 5.2. Continuing with the Patriots and Broncos example, the Patriots actually won the game by 34 points (41 points - 7 points). Your projected point spread, using the Value Ratings, forecast the Patriots to win by 12 points. Thus the difference between the predicted margin of victory and the actual margin of victory was 24 points (34 points - 12 points). Using Table 5.2, the Value Adjustment Factor for each team would be 4 because the difference between the actual margin of victory and the predicted margin of victory was between 20 and 24 points. So 4 would be added to the Patriots Value Rating and 4 would be subtracted from the Broncos Value Rating. Before their game with the Broncos, the Patriots had a Value Rating of 105, so after the game, the Value Rating for the Patriots would be raised to 109 (105 + 4 = 109). For the Broncos, their Value Rating would fall from 96 (their Value Rating before the game with the Patriots) to 92 after the game (96 - 4 = 92).

Table 5.2

Difference Between Predicted and Actual Margin of Victory	Value Adjustment Factor – Add for Winning Team/ Subtract for Losing Team
0 to 4 points	0
5 to 9 points	1
10 to 14 points	2
15 to 19 points	3
More than 20 points	4

Table 5.2 reports that if the margin of victory is within 4 points of your projection, then no change would be made to either team's Value Rating. If the margin of victory is within 5 and 9 points of your forecast, then the adjustment to each team's Value Rating would be 1. If it's 10 to 14 points away, adjust by 2 for each team. A difference of 15 points to 19 points would require an adjustment of 3 to each team's Value Rating. And if there is more than a 20-point difference, the adjustment would be 4 for each team.

Recall that Value Ratings are to be used as a "top-down" method to forecast point spreads. They provide a relative measure of the strength of each team, and you should update them weekly to gain a deeper understanding of how teams are doing as the season progresses — which teams are getting better and which teams are getting worse.

Above all, when adjusting your Value Ratings, understand that the mechanical adjustment method I have outlined is meant as a guide — not as gospel. Many random and unpredictable factors can influence the margin of victory for a game: weather, injuries, unusual plays. Since it is ultimately your own experience, knowledge and judgment that will determine your sports betting edge, you should evaluate all factors when determining the appropriate adjustment to each team's Value Rating.

Consider the NFL game played between the Saints and the Browns during Week Five of the 2010-11 season. The major Las Vegas and Internet sports books had the Saints as a 12-point favorite, but the underdog Browns stunned the favored Saints and won the game 30-17. An analysis of game statistics reveals that Drew Brees, the Saints quarterback, uncharacteristically threw four interceptions during the game — two of which were returned for touchdowns by the Browns. While a "pick six" is the kind of exciting play that fans love to see and usually has a significant impact on the outcome of a game, it is unusual and occurs infrequently, especially when it happens twice to an all-pro quarterback. According to Table 5.2, the adjustment to the Saints and Browns Value Ratings would be 4 (the actual adjustment would depend on your own calculated point spread for the game), but adding 4 to Browns Value Rating and lowering the Saints Value Rating by a corresponding amount is probably too extreme based on two plays that had a disproportionate impact on the game's result. Adjusting each team's Value Rating by 1 or 2 would be more appropriate.

Applying and Updating NBA Value Ratings

The Value Rating system for the NBA is similar to the NFL's. The same relative value ranking hierarchy holds true for the relationship between each of the 30 teams in the NBA, meaning that there are 30 fixed Value Ratings scale for the NBA and it is only the teams themselves that move around within the predetermined values throughout the season and from year to year. The Value Rating scale itself does not change. The highest rating for the NBA is 108 and the lowest rating is 91.

For the 2010-11 NBA season, the ending Value Ratings are reported in Table 5.3:

Table 5.3

NBA Value Ratings (2010-11) – Season End	
108	Dallas Mavericks
107	Miami Heat

106	Oklahoma City Thunder
106	Chicago Bulls
105	Boston Celtics
105	Los Angeles Lakers
104	San Antonio Spurs
104	Memphis Grizzlies
103	Atlanta Hawks
103	Portland Trail Blazers
102	Houston Rockets
102	New Orleans Hornets
101	Denver Nuggets
101	Orlando Magic
100	Phoenix Suns
100	Philadelphia 76ers
99	New York Knicks
99	Utah Jazz
99	Milwaukee Bucks
98	Golden State Warriors
98	Los Angeles Clippers

97	Charlotte Bobcats
96	Indiana Pacers
96	Sacramento Kings
96	Detroit Pistons
94	New Jersey Nets
94	Toronto Raptors
94	Washington Wizards
92	Cleveland Cavaliers
91	Minnesota Timberwolves

As with the NFL, to make predictions for upcoming games, simply compare the ratings of the teams playing in the game. But for the NBA, add 3.5 more points to the home team's Value Rating (instead of 3 points for the NFL) to reflect the statistically significant home field advantage. For example, a home team with a Value Rating of 105 (the Los Angeles Lakers in Table 5.3) would be favored by 6.5 points over a visiting team having a Value Rating of 102 (the Houston Rockets in Table 5.3). Moreover, a visiting team with a Value Rating of 107 (the Miami Heat in Table 5.3) would be favored by 5.5 points when playing against a home team having a Value Rating of 98 (the Golden State Warriors in Table 5.3).

Consider an imaginary NBA game where the Los Angeles Lakers are hosting the Orlando Magic. The point spread posted by the sports books for the game is:

```
Orlando
Los Angeles    -9
```

Using the NBA Value Ratings in Table 5.3, Los Angeles is rated at 105 and Orlando is rated at 101. Los Angeles is the home team, so 3.5 points are added to Los Angeles' rating, making their at-home Value Rating 108.5 (105 + 3.5 = 108.5). Using the Value Ratings to determine the predicted outcome of the game, you simply subtract 108.5 from 101: 108.5 minus 101 equals 7.5. Therefore you would expect Los Angeles to win the game by 7.5 points, which is your predicted point spread for the game.

Next, compare your Value Rating forecast of the point spread to the sports book's posted point spread to determine if there is a substantial difference between your forecast and the point spread. In this example, the sports book's posted line says the Lakers are favored by 9 points. But your Value Rating forecast predicts that Los Angeles will win by 7.5 points. That means there is only a 1.5-point difference between the sports book's posted point spread and the Value Rating prediction, so it's probably best to pass on this wager because the Margin of Safety is too small.

Regardless of whether you bet on a game, you should still update your Value Ratings to reflect the outcome. Let's say the Magic upset the Lakers in this imaginary NBA game by the score of 101-97. To adjust your Value Ratings for each team, you simply compare the final score of the game to your projected point spread. Value Adjustment Factors for the NBA are shown in Table 5.4. Continuing with the Lakers and Magic imaginary example, the Magic won the game by 4 points (101-97). Your projected point spread, using the Value Ratings, forecast the Lakers to win by 7.5 points. Thus the difference between your predicted margin of victory and the actual margin of victory was 11.5 points. Using Table 5.4, the Value Rating Adjustment Factor for each team would be 1, so you add 1 to the Orlando Value Rating and subtract 1 from the Los Angeles Value Rating. Before the game with the Lakers, the Magic had a Value Rating of 101; after the game, the Value Rating for the Magic would be raised to 102 (101 + 1 = 102). For the Lakers, their Value Rating would fall from 105 before the game with the Magic to 104 after the game (105 - 1 = 104).

Table 5.4

Difference Between Predicted and Actual Margin of Victory	Value Adjustment Factor – Add for Winning Team/ Subtract for Losing Team
0 to 4 points	0
5 to 12 points	1
More than 13 points	2

Table 5.4 also reports that if the margin of victory is within 4 points of your projection, then no change would be made to either team's Value Rating. If the margin of victory is within 5 to 12 points of your forecast, then the adjustment to each team's Value Rating would be 1. If the margin of victory is more than 13 points different from your forecast, then the adjustment to each team's Value Rating would be 2.

With the Value Rating, You Are 80 Percent of the Way There

Have you ever heard of the 80/20 Rule? Also known as the Pareto Principle, it was developed in 1906 by economist Vilfredo Pareto. His principle says that the first 80 percent of any undertaking can be accomplished with 20 percent of the effort, assuming you have the proper knowledge and the right tools. What a motivator! Pareto says that if you know what you are doing and have a plan, you can get 80 percent of the results by doing 20 percent of the work. The value of the Pareto Principle is that it reminds you to focus on the 20 percent that matters most.

The Value Rating is an application of the Pareto Principle because a well-thought-out set of Value Ratings provides 80 percent of the necessary game analysis with 20 percent of the effort. A corollary to the Pareto

Principle is Occam's Razor,[27] which is attributed to the 14th-century English theologian and Franciscan friar William Ockham (yes, his name is spelled differently than his discovery). The gist of Occam's Razor is that the simpler the solution, the more likely it is to be correct. The simple, yet accurate, *Get In and Win* Value Rating is the first step in your game analysis, with a few more to go before you have a complete understanding of how to identify on which side of the point spread value lies. Recreational bettors looking for a sensible way to just do better than the average fan may want to stop at the Value Rating level of analysis, but those who are after the big rewards will want to go further.

While Value Ratings can get you a long way toward your objective, they are more of a blunt instrument than a precise cutting tool. Think of it this way: A Value Rating is the road map you would use to get from your house to the stadium for the game. Once inside the arena, you need something more exact so you can find your seat. You need a more detailed guide (something I call a Score Sheet) because it is in the last 20 percent where you can really increase your Win Rate and get big winnings on the Scorecard.

Wall Street Uses DuPont Analysis

When analyzing stocks on Wall Street, many professional investors use a technique called DuPont Analysis to drill deeper into the elements influencing corporate profitability. There are five factors that determine how much money a company will make: (1) asset turnover; (2) operating margins; (3) amount of debt; (4) interest rate paid on debt; and (5) effective income tax rate. By breaking corporate financial performance into distinct parts and focusing on the individual pieces, professional analysts can evaluate how effectively a company is using its assets, leading them to identify investment opportunities that are not apparent to less sophisticated investors.

---

27 A razor is a heuristic or commonsense "rule of thumb" that philosophers use to shave away unlikely explanations in order to speed up the process of solving a problem.

The *Get In and Win* Score Sheets were developed to provide sports bettors with a tool similar to DuPont Analysis. In the same way, Score Sheets separate the elements that determine the number of points a team will score into distinct pieces so sports bettors can get a better understanding of the factors influencing team performance. With that information, the Intelligent Bettor has an advantage over his competition — the general betting public.

Score Sheets Put You in the Winning Seat

The Score Sheet lets you drill into the detail and analyze the individual factors that determine the *score* of a game with just a few simple inputs. That's right, the Score Sheets provide a step-by-step method to forecast the *total points* that each team will score in a game. Once the number of points each team is projected to score is known, then the point spread can be calculated (as well as some other Hidden Treasures that are described in Chapter Nine).

With the results of the Score Sheet in hand, you can verify and think about any adjustments you might want to make to your Value Rating determined point spread. Recall that the point spread forecast derived using Value Ratings is a top-down look at the game, while the Score Sheet provides a detailed bottom-up view. Combining the Value Rating framework with the Score Sheet gives you the benefit of both perspectives on the game. Use the Value Ratings to get to the stadium and the Score Sheet to confirm that you are in a winning seat.

There are proprietary *Get In and Win* Score Sheets for each of the major sports: college and professional football; college and professional basketball; and Major League Baseball. Just as with the Value Ratings, the Score Sheets are explained in more detail in each of the separate *Get In and Win* Playbooks. The Score Sheets are based on extensive research published by statistical experts who have studied football, basketball and baseball in great detail for years. For the NFL and college football, the Score Sheets use models introduced by David Berri and Martin Schmidt in their best-selling book, *The Wages of Wins*.[28] The Score Sheets for the NBA and college basketball are based on the combined efforts of Dean Oliver (*Basketball on Paper*) and Wayne Winston (*Mathletics*).[29] And Major League Baseball's Score Sheet is an extension of the methods described by the legendary Branch Rickey in his article "Good-Bye to Some Old Baseball Ideas" (published by *Life* magazine in 1954) and further refined by Eric Walker.[30]

Fantasy Fanatics Love the NFL Score Sheets

OK, this is just what all of you fantasy sports fanatics have been waiting for. The Score Sheets let you put to use all that knowledge you have been accumulating over the years about your favorite players and teams to make a profit for you. Based on some sophisticated statistical and economic modeling techniques, the easy-to-use Score Sheets are designed so that you can plug in the relevant statistics and out pops an accurate prediction of the number of points each team will score in a game. And best of all, you don't have to do the regression arithmetic because the Score Sheets do it for you. You simply use your knowledge of the teams and players to come up with the required inputs, and then work through a few simple computations to forecast the number of points each team will score. To understand how Score Sheets work, we will review examples from the NFL and NBA.

---

28 Berri is an associate professor of applied economics at California State University and Schmidt is a professor of economics at the College of William and Mary. They maintain a website, www.wagesofwins.com, and their writing on sports appears frequently in *The New York Times*.

29 Oliver was most recently the director of performance analytics for the Denver Nuggets and Winston is professor of Decision Sciences at Indiana University's Kelly School of Business. Winston also serves as a consultant for the Dallas Mavericks.

30 Rickey, an innovative baseball executive with the St. Louis Cardinals and Brooklyn Dodgers, was elected into the Baseball Hall of Fame in 1967 and is probably best known for creating baseball's minor league system. Walker, an engineer by training, was a pioneer in sports analytics; his early efforts inspired Billy Beane's quantitative approach to baseball as described in Michael Lewis' best-seller *Moneyball*.

Starting with the NFL: To predict the number of points each team will score in a game, you just need to make an informed estimate of the following seven items for each of the teams playing in the game:

> Rushing attempts
> Net rushing yards
> Passing attempts
> Net passing yards
> Fumbles
> Interceptions thrown $\rangle$ TOs, TAs
> Missed field goals

Now, the fantasy fanatics can get very detailed and use the estimated individual performances of each player to come up with the total for each category, but that is not really necessary. It's up to you to determine whether incorporating individual player performance improves your forecasting accuracy.

When I manage an investment portfolio, my principal consideration is properly allocating the precious investment capital that has been entrusted to my care. The amount of money that any investor has is limited. Thus it is paramount to deploy the capital carefully to maximize investment returns while minimizing risk. Plays in a football game can be viewed in the same way as investment capital. Those plays are precious because they are limited in number, so coaches should "spend" them carefully.

The economic theory behind allocating scarce, valuable investment capital forms the basis for the *Get In and Win* NFL Score Sheets, with offensive plays serving as the underlying currency and points earned being the economic measurement unit. Passing and rushing plays represent a *charge* or *use of capital*, with each passing play being assigned a negative value because the play consumes a resource (there are 63 offensive plays in the average NFL game — 37 passing plays[31] and 26 rushing plays). Moreover, a passing play can have an additional negative impact because the game clock stops on incomplete passes, which allows more time for the opposing team to possess the ball and provides additional opportunities for the opponent to score.

---

31 In the *Get In and Win* System, sacks are considered passing plays.

Thus, passing plays *cost* a negative .33 points per play. On the other hand, while a rushing play also represents a *spent* play, the game clock usually continues to run after the rushing play is completed, which has the benefit of *reducing* the amount of time the opponent can possess the ball. For rushing plays, the value received from keeping the game clock winding down more than compensates for the negative *spending* associated with using the play, so rushing plays have a positive value in the *Get In and Win* model. Thus, rushing plays are rewarded and are credited at a positive .07 points per play.

Since the basic purpose of rushing and passing plays is to advance the ball while attempting to score points, a point value can also be determined and assigned to each rushing yard and passing yard. Rushing yards have a value of .08 points per yard. Because more bad things can happen on a pass play (sack, interception, incompletion) than on a running play, pass plays are more risky — but when a pass is completed the average total yards gained are more than for the average running play. Thus, pass plays are higher-risk but higher-reward and are assigned a value of .10 points per yard. Table 5.5 summarizes the point values associated with running plays, passing plays and yards gained:

Table 5.5

	Rushing	Passing
Play Value	.07 points per play	-.33 points per play
Yardage Value	.08 points per yard	.10 points per yard

Finally, any experienced NFL fan can tell you that turnovers significantly influence game outcomes. Here's why: in the average NFL game, each team has approximately 12 possessions, or *drives*, so each drive is extremely valuable. Every turnover committed (fumble and interception) or missed field goal uses up one of the 12 scoring opportunities with no points earned. To make matter worse, giveaways provide the opponent with an additional chance to score. The *Get In and Win* Score Sheet values for turnovers and missed field goals are reported in Table 5.6:

Table 5.6

	Giveaways	Takeaways
Interceptions	-1.6 points	3.1 points
Fumbles	-2.1 points	1.9 points
Missed Field Goals	-4.2 points	N/A

Consider the 2011 NFL Wild Card that was played between the Green Bay Packers and the Philadelphia Eagles. The relevant game statistics for the *Get In and Win* NFL Score Sheet appear in Table 5.7 (everything else can be disregarded):

Table 5.7

	Green Bay	Philadelphia
Rushing Attempts	32	21
Net Rushing Yards	138	81
Passing Attempts	29	39
Net Passing Yards	171	271
Interceptions Thrown	0	1
Fumbles	2	0
Missed Field Goals	0	2

Using the *Get In and Win* forecasting method for the NFL, the Packers would have been projected to score 20 points and the Eagles would have been projected to score 16 points, as shown on Score Sheet 5.8. The Packers actually won the game 21-16. The point spread for the game had

Philadelphia as the favorite and the posted line was Philadelphia -6. Most sports books posted the *total* wager for the game at 46.5 (which is the combined final score for both teams).[32] If you had properly predicted the game statistics, you would have gladly taken the points and placed a wager on the underdog Packers — and you would have bet the "under" on the total. Both of your bets would have been winners. Of course, there is no money to be made calculating the score of a game *after* it has been played. The point of the exercise is to demonstrate the accuracy of the Score Sheet method using statistics from an actual NFL game and a real-life betting line.

Score Sheet 5.8

NFC Wild Card Game
January 9, 2011

	Green Bay Packers				Philadelphia Eagles			
Rushing		Factor Value	Projected Points	Play Avg		Factor Value	Projected Points	Play Avg
Rushing Plays	33	0.07	2.3		21	0.07	1.5	
Yards	138	0.08	11.0	4.3	81	0.08	6.5	3.9
Rushing Points			13.3				8.0	
Passing								
Passing Plays	29	−0.33	−9.6		39	−0.33	−12.9	
Yards	171	0.10	17.1	5.9	271	0.10	27.1	6.9
Passing Points			7.5				14.2	
Give Aways								
Interceptions	0.0	−1.6	0.0		1.0	−1.6	−1.6	
Fumbles	2.0	−2.1	−4.2		0.0	−2.1	0.0	
Missed FGs	0.0	−4.2	0.0		2.0	−4.2	8.4	
Giveaway Points			−4.2				−10.0	
Take Aways								
Interceptions	1.0	3.1	3.1		0.0	3.1	0.0	
Fumbles	0.0	1.9	0.0		2.0	1.9	3.8	
Takeaway Points			3.1				3.8	
Projected Total Points			20				16	

---

32 Total wagers are described in Chapter Nine.

The NBA Score Sheet

For the NBA Score Sheet, the first thing to consider is the game tempo: Will it be fast, slow or somewhere in between? Having a sense of the tempo enables you to make a sensible estimate of the number of scoring opportunities that each team will have.[33] In the previous section presenting the NFL Score Sheet, you learned that plays serve as the underlying currency when applying an economic model to an NFL game. For the NBA, it's possessions that serve as the base unit of value for the Score Sheet. Like plays in the NFL, possessions in the NBA are a precious and valuable resource; they should be used wisely.

After considering game tempo, you will need to make an informed forecast of the following seven factors that affect the performance of each team and the outcome of a basketball game:

> Offensive Rebounds
> Turnovers
> 2-Point Shot Attempts
> 2-Point Field Goal Percentage
> 3-Point Shot Attempts
> 3-Point Field Goal Percentage
> Free Throw Percentage

(handwritten notes:)

Heat
Possessions
72
- 9
63
+ 16
79 + (0.475 × 16) = 86.6

As an example of how the NBA Score Sheet works, let's review Game Six, which turned out to be the final game, of the 2010-11 NBA Finals between the Dallas Mavericks and the Miami Heat. For that game, the relevant statistics for the *Get In and Win* Score Sheet are presented in Table 5.9:

(handwritten notes:)

82   Mavs
-10   Possessions
72
+14
86 + (0.475 × 18) = 94.55

---

33 The NBA Playbook contains a detailed explanation of game tempo and explains why the possessions are equal for each of the two teams playing in an NBA game.

Table 5.9

Game Factor	Dallas	Miami
Possessions	95	95
Offensive Rebounds	10	9
Turnovers	14	16
2-Point Attempts	56	49
2-Point Field Goal Percentage	53.6%	55.1%
3-Point Attempts	26	23
3-Point Field Goal Percentage	42.3%	30.4%
Free Throw Percentage	66.7%	60.6%

Score Sheet 5.10 shows a *Get In and Win* analysis of the game: 5/

Score Sheet 5.10

NBA Championship
June 12, 2011

	DALLAS	MIAMI
Possessions/Tempo	95	95
Offensive Rebounds	10	9
Turnovers	14	16
Scoring Opportunities Available # of Shots	91	88

Scoring Opportunities		Percent successful	Number used	Number of points		Percent successful	Number used	Number of points
3 Point Attempts	26		26		23		23	
3 Point Made	11	42.3%		33	7	30.4%		21
2 Point Attempts	56		56		49		49	
2 Point Made	30	53.6%		60	27	55.1%		54
Free Throw Attempts	18 $X \cdot 5 =$		9		33		16	
Free Throws Made	12	66.7%		12	20	60.6%		20
Scoring Opportunities Used			91				88	
Total Number of Points				105				95

What? All you did was total up the number of points from an already played game!!

Using the Score Sheet forecasting method for the NBA and the actual statistics from the game, the Mavericks would have been projected to score 105 points and the Heat would have been projected to score 95 points. The Mavericks won the game 105-95, supporting the accuracy of the NBA Score Sheet.

The first step in completing the *Get In and Win* NBA Score Sheet is to estimate the number of possessions for the game, which serves as the starting point for determining the number of scoring opportunities for each team. In the Mavericks versus Heat game, the number of possessions was 95.[34] Next we identify the primary actions taken by each team on the court and evaluate how those actions affected the game's outcome. The events that occur during a basketball game can be grouped into two primary categories: (1) actions affecting possession of the basketball; and (2) attempts to score. Drilling down further, the items impacting possessions are offensive rebounds and turnovers. Scoring opportunities can be broken down into 2-point field goal attempts, 3-point field goal attempts and free throw attempts.

Offensive rebounds are positive adjustments to possessions because offensive rebounds result in additional opportunities to score — making offensive rebounds highly valuable. In this game, the Mavericks had 10 offensive rebounds and the Heat had nine. The second game factor influencing possessions is turnovers. Turnovers are a negative adjustment to possessions because turnovers eliminate scoring opportunities. Dallas committed 14 turnovers and the Heat committed 16 in this game.

After accounting for the factors that happen during a basketball game that only affect possessions (offensive rebounds and turnovers), the remaining NBA Score Sheet analysis focuses on scoring opportunities: how each team chooses to use them and how successful each team is in converting its scoring opportunities into points. As reported on the Score Sheet in the row labeled Scoring Opportunities Available, the Mavericks had 91 opportunities to score and the Heat had 88 in this game. The Mavericks used their 91 scoring opportunities as follows: 56 were spent on 2-point field goal

---

34 To determine the number of possessions for each team in a basketball game, use this equation: Possessions = Field Goals Attempted - Offensive Rebounds + Turnovers + (0.475 x Free Throws Attempted).

attempts, 26 were spent on 3-point field goal attempts and nine were spent getting to the free throw line. On the other hand, the Heat used their 88 scoring opportunities as follows: 49 possessions were spent on 2-point field goal attempts, 23 were spent on 3-point field goal attempts and 16 were spent getting to the free throw line.

It's interesting that the Mavericks had three more scoring opportunities in this game because they had two more offensive rebounds and one less turnover than the Heat. From this analysis, it's clear that the Mavericks won this game because they had more scoring opportunities and they were more successful and efficient in converting their scoring opportunities into points. The Mavericks used their scoring possessions to shoot 2- and 3-point field goals, and they were successful at converting a relatively high percentage (53.6 percent of 2-point attempts and 42.3 percent of 3-point attempts). While the Heat did a good job of converting their 2-point attempts (55.1 percent) and getting to the foul line, they failed to convert their free-throw opportunities into points because they shot a relatively low percentage, 60.6 percent, from the charity stripe.

As Score Sheet 5.10 demonstrates, using your knowledge to accurately complete the *Get In and Win* NBA Score Sheet will produce a prediction for the outcome of the game that will be exactly the final score. The ball is now in your court to properly evaluate each game matchup, come up with the appropriate inputs, and rack up some sports betting wins.

Check the Alignment

You now have two ways to calculate your own point spread for any sporting event and find value in the betting lines: The first uses Value Ratings and the second uses the Score Sheet method. Value Ratings provide a broad-brush or top-down view of the strength of each team. The Value Rating summarizes a lot of information in a single number. On the other hand, the Score Sheet provides its own special perspective by looking at a game from the bottom up and examining the game statistics that are most relevant in determining points scored. What you are looking for is alignment between the results of both methods. You will rarely have an exact match, but you need them to be in balance.

Recall that a substantial difference between the sports book's posted point spread and your predicted outcome of the game is what you are seeking. Alignment gives you the confidence to act decisively when you spot that difference.

If your point spread prediction using Value Ratings is not comparable to your Score Sheet calculation, you should carefully examine your inputs and assumptions for each. That way you are constantly testing and refining your opinions about the capabilities of each team as you try to bring the Value Ratings and Score Sheets into alignment. While *Get In and Win* provides you with a reliable valuation framework to get an edge, it is ultimately your own knowledge and judgment that will determine whether there is alignment between the Value Rating predictions and your Score Sheet forecasts. If after careful consideration you are unable to get them in balance for a particular game and you don't believe additional adjustments are called for, don't despair — just don't bet. Recall that in Chapter Three you learned there are no called strikes in sports wagering, so the only way you can make an out is to swing and miss. When there is no alignment, pass and move on, because placing a bet when you don't have an edge increases your chances of striking out.

Alignment and Margin of Safety — A Powerful Combination

Now we are ready to examine where the real money is made. Once you have found those games where there is alignment between the point spread forecast using your Value Ratings and Score Sheets, you are ready to compare your point spread forecast to the line posted by the sports book. You are looking for those games where there is a significant difference between the point spread you have calculated and the posted line. Remember, as discussed throughout this book, the posted line is not the sports book's prediction for the game. The posted line only represents the point spread necessary to evenly divide the wagering action and allow the sports book to balance its books.

As discussed in Chapter Four, the difference between your calculated point spread and the posted line is the Margin of Safety — and the bigger the difference, the larger the Margin of Safety. You should bet only when there is a comfortable Margin of Safety. The appropriate Margin of Safety is tricky to assess and is a function of your overall judgment as an Intelligent Bettor. While there is no exact numerical threshold for determining a suitable Margin of Safety, my experience on Wall Street tells me that you want at least a 15 percent Margin of Safety in order to place an actual wager and risk your precious capital.

In the NFL and NBA Playbooks, there are complete Margin of Safety Cheat Sheets. The Margin of Safety Cheat Sheet tells you the actual Margin of Safety, expressed in numerical terms, between your point spread forecast and the posted line, so that you don't have to actually calculate it. The Margin of Safety Cheat Sheet was derived from the risk control calculations the sports books themselves use when setting their lines[35] and is a very handy reference tool.

An example is the best way to learn to how to use the Margin of Safety Cheat Sheet. Let's imagine an NFL football game between the New England Patriots and the New York Giants. You have performed your *Get In and Win* game analysis, checked the alignment between your Value Rating and Score Sheet forecasts and determined that the Giants should be 3-point favorites. That means you have priced the game at New York -3. The posted line is New York -7. The 4-point difference between your forecast and the posted line indicates that the Giants are overvalued by the betting public and the Patriots are undervalued. Now the key question becomes: Is the Margin of Safety related to this 4-point difference large enough to place a wager on the Patriots?

Table 5.11 presents the relevant part of the Margin of Safety Cheat Sheet from the NFL Playbook. Referring to Table 5.11, we find that the Margin of Safety between your forecasted line of -3 and a posted line of -7 is 25 percent (look down the -3 column and across the -7 row and you will find the number 25 in the box where the specified row and column meet).

---

35 As described by Michael Roxborough, founder of Las Vegas Sports Consultants, in his book *Sports Book Management – A Guide for the Legal Bookmaker.* Since 1985, the opening lines published by Las Vegas Sports Consultants have served as the industry standard for sports books to use when establishing their own point spreads.

Table 5.11   Margin of Safety Cheat Sheet (% Difference)

	Predicted Line									
Posted Line	-2.0	-2.5	-3.0	-3.5	-4.0	-4.5	-5.0	-6.0	-6.5	-7.0
-2.0		3	8	10	15	18	20	23	25	27
-2.5	3		5	7	13	15	17	20	22	24
-3.0	9	5		2	8	10	13	16	18	20
-3.5	12	8	2		6	8	11	14	16	18
-4.0	18	14	8	6		3	5	9	11	13
-4.5	22	18	12	9	3		3	6	8	11
-5.0	25	21	15	12	6	3		3	6	8
-6.0	29	25	19	16	9	6	4		3	5
-6.5	33	29	22	19	12	9	6	3		3
-7.0	36	32	25	22	15	12	9	5	3	

This means that New England can play 25 percent worse than your forecast before you lose the bet. Another way to look at it is that New England can absorb a number of unanticipated negative factors such as injuries, unanticipated turnovers, bad bounces, lucky plays, etc., before causing you to lose your bet on the Patriots. Since a 25 percent Margin of Safety is greater than our 15 percent threshold requirement, you should place a bet on New England.

A Replay of the Playbook for Finding Value

In much the same way that sports teams consider intelligent scouting and analysis as vital to their long-term success, finding value is what it takes to consistently make winning wagers. The steps for finding value in the sports betting line are summarized below:

➤ Step 1 - Develop a set of Value Ratings to get an objective assessment of the strength of each team and to predict the point spread differential between teams.

➤ **Step 2** - Use the Score Sheet to project the score of a specific game using your best estimate of certain game statistics. With the Score Sheet's projection of the number of points each team is expected to score in hand, you have another tool to establish a point spread for a game.

➤ **Step 3** - To set your own final forecast for the point spread, apply your own knowledge and judgment to align the Value Rating and Score Sheet projections for the point spread.

➤ **Step 4** - Compare your forecasted point spread for the game to the sports book's posted point spread.

➤ **Step 5** - Determine if an adequate Margin of Safety exists between your forecasted line and the sports book's posted line. If the Margin of Safety is reasonable, place your wager. If it is unsatisfactory, pass and move on to analyzing the next bet.

While consistently applying this systematic approach requires a great deal of discipline and focus, it is worth following because the *Get In and Win* step-by-step process enables you to selectively identify winning bets and avoid losing ones. A proper assessment of value and the ability to be selective are powerful tools that put the opportunity to make a lot of money within your grasp. But, like Cinderella at the ball, you must heed one important warning or everything will turn into pumpkins and mice — you must practice careful money management, the benefits of which are discussed thoroughly in the next chapter. So please turn the page and read on before placing your wagers.

The Money Management Game Plan

"Money won is twice as sweet as money earned."

Paul Newman
The Color of Money

Wagering on sports can be exciting, rewarding — and stressful. Ironically, the uncertainty associated with the outcome of a bet makes wagering on sports both exhilarating and anxiety-inducing. The psychology associated with winning and losing streaks, and having the proper money management plan to get you through the emotional highs and lows, are the most underappreciated aspects of sports wagering. Being aware of both is critical because there are opportunities for profit even when things seem the most difficult.

Effective money management is about balancing the need to maximize the number of winning bets while limiting the loss of your precious sports betting capital. The Money Management Game Plan presented as part of the *Get In and Win* System is a simple and sensible method that enhances your profits, reduces your risk of loss and allows you to stay in the game so you can keep making winning bets. The Intelligent Bettor has a good understanding of psychology and has a predetermined Money Management Game Plan in place. He is able to control his emotions and focus on his game analysis regardless of whether he is experiencing that euphoric feeling that comes with winning bets or facing the self-doubt associated with the inevitable losing streak.

Keep It Simple and Be Selective

Money management does not involve sophisticated accounting or financial systems, or complicated progressive wagering schemes. It is simply the disciplined application of a few basic fundamentals about when and how much to wager. Every professional investor knows that the first rule of making money is not to lose it. This is the first rule for the Intelligent Bettor as well. While it is impossible to win all of your sports bets, careful money management begins with never placing more of your capital at risk than you can afford to lose. Limiting your bet sizes protects against the risk of a single loss wiping you out.

Start by separating your sports betting capital from your personal money. If you plan to bet seriously, your sports betting capital should not be money that is needed for personal expenditures. Do not bet the mortgage, rent or grocery money. Remember: Your betting capital has to be money you don't mind losing. If it's needed for something critical, then it no longer fulfills that criterion.

Next, be selective. As discussed in Chapter Three, approach each wagering opportunity like Ted Williams getting ready to hit a baseball — swing only at pitches that are in your hitting zone and where you have an adequate Margin of Safety. Place your wagers on the best opportunities and pass on games where you have no advantage.

How Much to Bet: The Five Percent Rule

At the heart of the Money Management Game Plan is the Five Percent Rule: There is one and only one appropriate bet size for each wager that you will make. That amount is an absolute fixed dollar amount and is calculated at the beginning of each season and stays fixed at that level for the entire season.[36] *The appropriate bet size is 5 percent of your beginning sports wagering capital.*

For example, if you begin the season with $1,000 of sports wagering capital, then the appropriate size for each wager is $50 — no more, no less. If you begin the season with $5,000, the appropriate wager size is $250 per bet, and if you start with $10,000, it is $500 per bet. Maintaining a fixed bet size that is equal to 5 percent of your beginning sports betting capital will prudently diversify your bets while producing generous returns at an acceptable level of risk. This is where most sports bettors fail. *The biggest single mistake made by most sports bettors is constantly changing the size of their bets.*

That's a strategy guaranteed to cost you money, unnecessarily depleting your capital. It does not matter whether the different bet sizes are a result of a panic-induced need to try to recover some difficult losses, a reaction to an extended winning streak, or part of a progressive betting scheme — don't do it. Have the discipline to follow the Five Percent Rule and bet an absolute fixed amount on each and every wager.

Not Too High and Not Too Low, but Just Right

The Intelligent Bettor has done the math. He has filled out his Scorecard. He knows the significant returns that can be earned if he sticks with his plan through thick and thin. The Intelligent Bettor knows that wipeouts are a financial disaster. He understands that if he suffers a 50 percent loss on his money he has to earn 100 percent just to get back to even. He views his sports betting capital as precious and he consistently bets 5 percent of his beginning sports betting capital on each wager.

Wagering a consistent 5 percent of your beginning capital properly diversifies your wagers, enhances your returns and limits the amount that you can lose on any one wager. A fixed-dollar bet size of 5 percent of your beginning wagering capital is high enough to produce a suitable return on your

---

36 Managing your wagers from the perspective of an investor seeking compound returns or a business owner looking to generate cash flow is discussed in detail in Chapter Eight.

investment, but it is not so high that it knocks you out of the game when you have a losing week. *Five percent is not too high and not too low, but just right.*

Money Mistakes

Poor money management generates more losses for players than bad game analysis. Even the worst bettors seldom lose on more than 55 percent of their picks, but they often lose most or all of their money.

The four most common money management errors when wagering on sports all involve changing bet sizes:

1. **Raising bet amounts.** Alan is a $100 bettor. He typically plays half a dozen or so games a week and is a dedicated sports bettor. The first week he makes five wagers of $110 to win $100 and goes 4-1, a fantastic Win Rate of 80 percent. For the week, he has made a profit of $290 (four wins of $100 and one loss of $110), a great week by any standard. He now thinks his wagering skills are so superior that he can consistently maintain a Win Rate of 80 percent, so he raises his bet size to $200. In the second week he makes six bets of $220 to win $200. Unfortunately, this week things don't work out so well and he goes 2-4. For the week he has lost $480 (two wins of $200 and four losses of $220). Over the course of two weeks, Alan has lost $190 despite an overall Win Rate of 54.5 percent. If he had simply played $110 on all 11 games, he would have made $50 in profit.

2. **Lowering bet amounts.** Bill is also a $100 bettor, but he is less confident than Alan. He makes six bets of $110 and goes 2-4 for a loss of $240 (two wins of $100 and four losses of $110). Because of the losing week, he cuts his bet size in half for the second week, making five wagers of just $55 to win $50 each. But this week he wins four out of five and makes $145 (four wins of $50 and one loss of $55). He now has the same overall winning record as Alan (6-5) and the same overall Win Rate of 54.5 percent, but he's down $95.

3. **Risking it all.** Charlie likes to take big risks for big rewards. He has $110 and risks it all on a single Saturday night game, which he wins. His betting capital is now $210 and he bets it all on a Sunday

1 p.m. game, which he also wins, bringing his betting capital to just over $400. Feeling lucky, he puts the whole amount on a 4 p.m. game and wins again, upping his betting capital to an incredible $765 in less than a day. Then he decides to go for the big win and goes "all in" on the Sunday night game, which he loses. Charlie has now lost it all despite going 3-1. Wagering $110 for each of the four games would have yielded a profit of $190.

4. **Chasing losses.** David has sports betting capital of $2,000. He wagers $110 on a game and loses. He is frustrated at losing the money and wants to win it back, so he wagers $121 (to win $110) on a second game and loses as well. He is now down $231 and is really frustrated. Convinced he can't lose three in a row, he wagers $254.10 (to win $231) and loses yet again. He has now lost $485.10. Even a win with his remaining betting capital of $514.90 won't get him back to even, but he puts it all in play on another game anyway, hoping to come close to breakeven (it would be a win of $468.09). He loses the fourth game and has busted out. Losing streaks will happen to every bettor every year, no matter how good he is, and those who chase their losses will not last long.

Get Up Enough Shots

Be wary of short-term results, whether good or bad. Most sports bettors make the mistake of evaluating their results over too short a period. They believe having a 65 percent Win Rate means winning six or seven out of every 10 bets in a perfect sequence, over and over again. Unfortunately, this is probably not going to happen — and even if it does, you can't bank on it. Financial advisors like myself deal with this kind of short-term thinking all the time — the retired client who thinks if his nest egg earned 15 percent last year, he can spend 15 percent of his nest egg this year. It's all gravy, right? Wrong! The problem is that his nest egg is highly unlikely to earn 15 percent two years in a row; this year it might actually *lose* money. Ouch! So that 15 percent gain has to last more than one year, maybe several years. Short-term thinking can kill you in retirement, and in sports betting.

Likewise, with a 65 percent Win Rate you are almost every bit as likely to go 8-12 one week as you are to go 18-2 the next. The consolation is that an 8-12 record one week combined with an 18-2 record the following week totals 26-14, which equals your expected Win Rate of 65 percent. It's similar to investors who successfully use a buy-and-hold strategy when managing their stocks. Buy-and-hold investors are not concerned with short-term price movements but instead look ahead, focusing on favorable company fundamentals to generate long-term profits. However, even with an effective buy-and-hold strategy there will be periods of time when an investor will lose money because of overall market downturns, causing some to foolishly dump their stocks at the wrong time. But when the long haul is a path you can comfortably take with your finances, then the buy-and-hold approach will almost surely net an acceptable return, assuming you have selected your stocks carefully.

To better understand the importance of getting enough betting opportunities, imagine two hypothetical basketball players: Sammy Swish and Arnold Airball. Sammy, the more skilled of the two, makes 65 percent of his free throw attempts. Arnold makes only 35 percent of his. Sammy and Arnold both enter a free throw shooting contest where two shooters are paired against each other, with only the winner of each pairing advancing to the next round. Sammy and Arnold play against each other in the first round. When reviewing the contest rules, Arnold and Sammy discover that each round involves only five shots, with the player making the most shots out of five advancing. Arnold, the poorer shooter, is very happy with the five-shot competition, but Sammy is disappointed because he was hoping that each round would involve at least a hundred shots. Why would the better player want more shots?

As any superior shooter in basketball knows, you have to keep shooting — even when you are missing — because skill will eventually kick in and the shots will start to fall. Since it is known before the competition begins that Sammy is a 65 percent shooter and Arnold is a 35 percent shooter, we can use some sophisticated binomial probability techniques to model the expected outcome of their matchup. The most likely outcome is that Sammy would be expected to successfully make three shots (65% x 5 shots) and Arnold to make two shots (35% x 5 shots). So it is expected that Sammy would win — but only by a small one-shot margin. However, that is only the *most likely* number of shots Sammy and Arnold are expected to make, among a number of other likely and not-so-likely results. In fact, Sammy is only somewhat more likely to make three shots out of five than he is to make two out of five. To make matters worse for Sammy, Arnold is only a bit less likely to make three out of five than he is to make two out of five. With just a small change in the likely outcomes, we could have Arnold Airball making three shots and Sammy Swish making two, which could cause Sammy, the better player, to go home the loser.

The problem, of course, is that five free throws are too few opportunities from which to draw any meaningful conclusions. You need a larger number in order to draw a valid conclusion. This is what statisticians call the *Rule of Large Numbers.* The rule says that when it comes to statistical certainty, the greater the number of observations, the more accurate the overall result. That explains why Billy Beane's A's have not won the World Series, even though they place high in the baseball standings almost every year — and why the ultimate World Series winner, or Super Bowl winner, cannot be predicted with absolute certainty, even when we know the two teams.

Because Sammy Swish is confident in his skill, he knows the Rule of Large Numbers is on his side in our imaginary free throw shooting contest: The more Sammy shoots, the more he will score.

The legendary football coach Bill Parcells likes to say, "You are what you are." But Coach Parcells only has it partially right. What he should say is, "You are what you are *if you have enough opportunities to prove it.*" Yogi Berra said it better when he remarked, "There ain't no lyin' over a 162-game season." And that's because playing 162 games provides enough opportunities to prove which players and teams are the best. For the Intelligent Bettor that means you have to make enough bets to demonstrate your sports wagering skill. You have to play the betting game in order to win the game. But with sports betting, there is an additional consideration. Your *shots* must be selectively chosen, high-quality bets.

The failure to understand the Rule of Large Numbers is the undoing of many sports bettors (and investors). Unfortunately, many bettors (and investors) don't or can't keep their eye on the long run. They become obsessed with the results of a particular game, or their win/loss record for each week, and react badly. To achieve success, sports wagering (and investing) must be viewed as an exercise in allocating capital over a long sequence of bets instead of a chance to win a one-time lottery jackpot.

To illustrate this point, Table 6.1 shows the range of wins and losses you can expect at various wagering levels,[37] assuming a 65 percent Win Rate:

Table 6.1   Expected Range of Wins and Losses

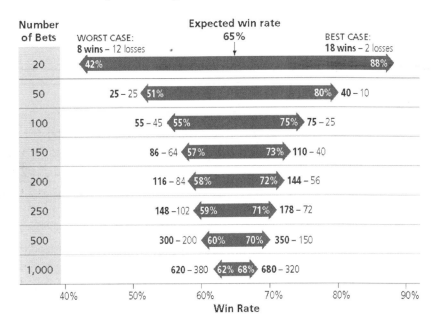

As you would expect knowing the Rule of Large Numbers, Table 6.1 reports that as the number of wagers increases, the range between the lowest and highest number of expected wins narrows, making it more likely that a sports bettor with a winning edge (in this instance a 65 percent Win Rate) will be a long-term winner. For example, assuming a 65 percent Win Rate after 50 wagers, Table 6.1 shows that a sports bettor would anticipate

---

37 Mathematicians know these return ranges (or variances) are a statistical certainty and refer to them in terms of *standard deviation*.

winning 32 or 33 of his wagers (50 wagers x 65%), but it is also equally likely that the number of wins could be in a range as low as 25 (51 percent Win Rate) and as high as 40 (80 percent Win Rate). After 500 wagers, the anticipated number of wins would be 325 (500 wagers x 65%) but could also fall anywhere within a range beginning as low as 300 wins (60 percent Win Rate) and as high as 350 wins (70 percent Win Rate) with an equal amount of certainty. At 1,000 bets, the chances for success for the skilled bettor increase even more, with a 62 percent Win Rate forming the low boundary of the expected win range.

Streaks

Another mathematical certainty associated with sports betting is that winning and losing streaks are guaranteed. They are a normal occurrence and there is no way to avoid them. Knowing that winning and losing streaks are coming makes them easier to deal with and get through. Or as the Buddha once said, "Don't get used to good conditions; don't get used to bad conditions."

To get a better understanding of winning and losing streaks, let's return to our basketball players, Sammy and Arnold. Recalling that Sammy is a 65 percent free throw shooter, Table 6.2 tells us that he has a 42 percent chance of making two shots in a row, a 27 percent chance of making three shots in a row, an 18 percent chance of making four shots in a row and a 12 percent chance of making all five shots. Table 6.2 also shows us that he also has a 12 percent chance of missing two shots in a row, a 4 percent chance of missing three shots in a row, a 2 percent chance of missing four shots in a row and a 1 percent chance of missing all five shots.

Table 6.2

Sammy Swish (65% shooter)

Makes in a Row	% Chance	Misses in a Row	% Chance
1	65%	1	35%
2	42%	2	12%
3	27%	3	4%
4	18%	4	2%
5	12%	5	1%

Arnold, however, is only a 35 percent shooter. So Table 6.3 tells us that he has just a 12 percent chance of making two shots in a row, a 4 percent chance of making three shots in a row, a 2 percent chance of making four shots in a row and a 1 percent chance of making all five shots. On the other hand, Table 6.3 reports that Arnold also has a 42 percent chance of missing two shots in a row, a 27 percent chance of missing three shots in a row, an 18 percent chance of missing four shots in a row and a 12 percent chance of missing all five shots.

Table 6.3

Arnold Airball (35% Shooter)

Makes in a Row	% Chance	Misses in a Row	% Chance
1	35%	1	65%
2	12%	2	42%
3	4%	3	27%
4	2%	4	18%
5	1%	5	12%

From these tables it is apparent that winning streaks occur more often for Sammy, the more skilled player. Because Sammy's chances of making five in a row are 12 percent, he should make five shots in a row about every eight sequences of shots (1/8 = 12%). On the other hand, Arnold's chances of making five in a row are only 1 percent, so Arnold is only going to hit five straight every 100 sequences (1/100 = 1%). The good news is that Tables 6.3 and Table 6.4 demonstrate that winning streaks happen more frequently for more skilled players because their opportunity for success is higher. The same holds true in sports betting — the greater your betting skill, the higher your Win Rate, and the more winning streaks you will have. Unfortunately, there is a bit of bad news in these tables: Even for skilled players, there will be losing streaks. And it's how you react to adversity caused by losing streaks that can ultimately determine your sports betting rewards.

But for now let's stay focused on the positives related to winning streaks and skill; because it gets even better the more shots you take as you become more skilled. Let's say Sammy takes 1,000 shots. Table 6.4 reports the number of times that he is likely to make five in a row at various shooting percentages.

Table 6.4

Streaks of Five Made Shots in Row
1,000 Shots

Shooting %	Occurrences of Five Made Shots in a Row
50%	6
55%	10
60%	16
65%	23
70%	34
75%	47
80%	66

So the more Sammy practices his free throws, the better he gets and the more times he will hit five in a row. Table 6.4 also tells us what would happen if Sammy could increase his free throw shooting percentage from 65 percent to 70 percent: He will increase the number of times that he is likely to make five in a row from 23 times out of 1,000 shots to 34 times. If you can do the same as a sports bettor, your profits will skyrocket too.[38] As Kevin Costner says in *Bull Durham*, "Know what the difference between hitting .250 and .300 is? It's 25 hits. Twenty-five hits in 500 at bats is 50 points, OK? There's six months in a season, that's about 25 weeks. That means if you get just one extra flare a week — just one — a gorp… you get a groundball, you get a groundball with eyes… you get a dying quail, just one more dying quail a week… and you're in Yankee Stadium."

It Hurts to Lose, and Here Is the Proof

If the arithmetic favors the skilled sports bettor, why is it that so few are successful at staying in the game? It's primarily because the losses hurt so much that the average bettor isn't psychologically prepared to work his way through them. To study the psychological affect that losses have, the noted economist Paul Samuelson[39] constructed an experiment in which he offered to pay some of his colleagues $200 if they correctly called heads or tails on a toss of a fair coin, and in return he would collect $100 for each incorrect call. Most people didn't accept the offer — even though they had a 1-in-2 chance of doubling their investment. The most common response was "I won't do it because I would feel the pain of the $100 loss more than the joy of the $200 gain, but I'll take you up on it if you promise to flip the coin 100 times."

What does this tell us about human behavior? It tells us that most people are averse to losses, because losses make us feel bad. In fact, when given a choice between two uncertain outcomes, most people are about two and a half times more averse to loss than they are happy about a comparable

---

38 If there is any doubt, take a look at the Scorecard examples in Chapter One.
39 Samuelson was the first American to win the Nobel Prize in Economic Sciences. He served as an advisor to Presidents John F. Kennedy and Lyndon B. Johnson.

gain — meaning that *they regret losses about two and a half times a much as they enjoy similar-size gains.*

Focusing on each single toss of the coin has yet another bad side effect. Placing too much emphasis on each flip causes people to become very short-term oriented. As a result, they tend to think about the losses more than wins, becoming even more risk averse. On the other hand, the less frequently they evaluate the results, the more likely they are to intuitively see gains when the odds are with them. That is why they elected to play when given the opportunity to toss the coin repeatedly, because they knew that over the long term the expected payoff was in their favor.

Why Zebras Don't Get Ulcers and Sports Bettors Do

In his book *Why Zebras Don't Get Ulcers*, brain researcher Robert Sapolsky makes the point that our bodies are sophisticated machines that have evolved over thousands of years. Our heritage can be traced back to the savannas of Africa, where, along with many other types of animals, our survival skills were honed. Sapolsky asks you to imagine a zebra grazing on the plain. Suddenly he is attacked by a lion. The zebra now has two choices — either try to defend himself against the lion's claws (a losing proposition) or run like crazy hoping that he can escape. Given this choice of "fight or flight," the zebra will always choose flight. His muscles are immediately flooded with energy, a boost that makes him far more able to escape the hungry lion.

For modern human beings, it doesn't work like that. We just sit around and worry. But in doing so, we turn on the same physiological responses that would occur if we were attacked by a lion. Our body floods with chemicals to help us to run, but we don't run; we don't use up those chemical resources. At this point, Sapolsky says, "our reactions become shortsighted, inefficient, and penny-wise and dollar-foolish."

Part of what makes sports betting fun and exciting is also what makes it stressful. Stress comes from a feeling of loss of predictability and control. *"I have had a streak of bad luck so I am due to win. And I have put in so much time analyzing these games that I think I will increase the size of my bets so I can make back some of my losses."* This type of stress-induced short-term thinking is common in sports wagering and can result in disaster. First, there is no such thing as being "due to win." Each wager is independent and unrelated to the previous wager. Second, remember that constantly changing the bet size is the biggest mistake most bettors make.

There Is Hope: Losing Is Part of Winning

The Intelligent Bettor recognizes when stress is creeping into his wagering activities. He controls it by maintaining his discipline and focusing on the proper process, not the results. He has accepted that there will inevitably be some losses, and he has come to grips with the feelings associated with losing. He knows that to be a winning sports bettor will ultimately involve some losing. He does not distract himself by evaluating his results too frequently. He is aware that a winning record is accumulated over the course of a season. Most of all he has confidence in the fact that he has prepared himself by doing his homework. Just as Phil Mickelson trusts his golf swing, the Intelligent Bettor has confidence in his money management plan and game analysis. And in the face of adversity and the stress that accompanies it, the Intelligent Bettor keeps his bet sizes at the predetermined fixed dollar amount (5 percent of his beginning sports betting capital) and stays selective, betting on only those games where he has a sufficient Margin of Safety.

In Case of Emergency, Do This

Every prudent money management program must have a contingency plan for extreme situations. It provides a safety valve should things go really badly. Since it is most important to have enough sports wagering capital to keep playing, you need to know what to do should you suffer some severe losses. While the Five Percent Rule is at the core of the *Get In and Win* System Money Management Game Plan, there is one exception to the principle of not changing your bet size. This occurs if, and only if, you ever reach the point where your sports betting capital is less than half the amount you began the season with. Extreme conditions demand extreme measures.

But guess what: That doesn't mean it's time to double down. In fact, it means just the reverse.

For example, if you started the season with $5,000 of sports betting capital and it falls below $2,500, then you should cut your fixed bet size in half. Continuing with this example, with $5,000 as beginning capital, your fixed bet size using the Five Percent Rule would be $250 ($5,000 x 5%). Should your available capital fall below $2,500, then reduce your bet size to $125. You should continue to wager at the reduced level until your capital level goes back above the emergency threshold of $2,500, at which point you should return to making $250 wagers.

It is important that this temporary reduction in bet size be implemented only in an emergency situation as a method to protect your sports wagering capital. Once you get back on the winning track, return your wagers to the standard 5 percent bet size.

Imitating Ulysses

Good money management will not make you a winner. Winning is a result of accurate game analysis, while effective money management is about properly balancing risk and return to maximize profits while limiting losses.

In Homer's epic *The Odyssey*, Ulysses longs to hear the Sirens' beautiful voices even though he knows that doing so will render him incapable of rational thought. To protect him from the call of the Sirens, Ulysses has his crew bind him to the ship's mast so that he won't jump in the water and drown. In the same way, sports bettors can also react irrationally, especially when experiencing that euphoric feeling that comes with placing a winning bet or riding a winning streak. Like Ulysses, sports bettors should take the steps necessary to focus on the significant financial rewards that can be achieved over time and ignore the short-term call of the Sirens.

To come out ahead in the long run, keep your wagers to reasonable, consistent amounts and make sure that you place enough high-quality bets to prove your skill. Recall that it is over time, not overnight, that you will earn real profits.

Reading the Line and Shopping for Value

How to Read the Board

Sports books have to cram a lot of information in a limited amount of space. To save "real estate" on the board, they post only the numbers and assume you know what they mean. Read this and you actually will.

This picture is from a typical Las Vegas casino sports book:

SUNDAY, OCT 11, 2009			**COLLEGE FOOTBALL**	
			SATURDAY, OCT 10, 20	9
N.F.L. WEEK #5				
401 VIKINGS	−10	−600	313 E.MICH.	
402 RAMS	41	+400	314 CENT MICH −23	
403 COWBOYS	−8	−400	315 DUKE	
404 CHIEFS	42.5	+300	316 N C STATE −16.5	3
405 REDSKINS	37.5	+165	317 MARYLAND	
406 PANTHERS	−3.5	−185	318 WK FOREST −12.5	
407 BUCCANEER			319 INDIANA	1
408 EAGLES	−14.5		320 VIRGINIA −7	
409 RAIDERS			321 PURDUE	
410 GIANTS	−15		322 MINN. −3	
411 BROWNS	41	+220	323 U CONN 46	
412 BILLS	−6	−300	324 PITT. −6.5	

Consider the first game in the upper left, which looks like this:

Oct. 11, 2009 — Vikings vs. Rams			
401	Vikings	-10	-600
402	Rams	41	+400

> ➤ 401 and 402 are the *rotation numbers*. These are just the numbers sports books give to each team or participant in a game or match. Every sports book uses the same rotation numbers for each game, so the rotation numbers for the Vikings and Rams game are the same at all Las Vegas casinos and across the Internet. This makes a lot of things easier, and helps avoid confusing your bet on the Arizona Cardinals with your bet on the St. Louis Cardinals.
> ➤ -10 is the point spread. This is for *point spread* wagers.
> ➤ 41 is the total points expected to be scored. This is for use in *total* bets.
> ➤ +400 and -600 are money lines. These are used in *money line* bets.

Point spreads, totals and money lines are the standard types of bets offered by sports books.

> ➤ **Point Spread Bets:** A point spread bet is a standard wager for or against the point spread, as discussed in Chapter Two.
> ➤ **Total Bets** Total bets are similar to point spread bets, except the bettor bets on the total points scored. In the example above, the wager is whether the total points combined between the Vikings and Rams will be over or under 41. Like point spread bets, the bettor must generally risk $11 to win $10. Totals can be profitable betting opportunities.[40]
> ➤ **Money Line Bets:** Money line bets are simply wagers on who will win straight up, without considering the point spread. The number represents the odds associated with each team's winning or losing

---

40 For more on total wagers, see Chapter Nine.

the game. In the example above, +400 for the Rams means that a $100 bet on the Rams would win $400 if the Rams win the game. The money line on the Vikings is -600, which means that the bettor must risk $600 to win $100. Played properly, money lines can be winning wagers.[41]

Let's take a moment and review what you learned in Chapter Two about a point spread bet before moving on to discussing why the line can change. In this example, the Vikings are favored to win by 10 points, so a couple of point spread bets would be available on this game: (1) that the Vikings will win by 11 or more points; or (2) that the Rams win or lose by 9 or fewer points. If the Vikings win by exactly 10, then point spread bets on both sides would "push," meaning there is no winner or loser and the amount wagered is returned to the bettors. Usually the point spread is displayed next to the favored team and is thus expressed as a negative number. The point spread is also referred to as *the line*.

To get the betting action started, sports books use a variety of methods to calculate their opening point spread. Most sports books use power ratings or some similar derivation. Some go further and use sophisticated computer programs that factor in historical betting action, recent performance, injuries, player matchups, etc. This allows them to make a more informed decision on whom the betting public will favor to win or lose and by how much. Once sports books make this decision, they use it to set their line *in a way that will best balance betting on both sides of the point spread and maximize betting action — not to reflect the likely outcome of the game.*

To win consistently, you must have a set of advantages that can compensate for the service charge paid to the sports book on each winning bet. (Remember that most point spreads are offered at standard odds of -110, meaning you must risk $110 to win $100. The $10 is the service charge.) Your primary advantage is that you don't have to wager on every game; you can pick and choose your wagering opportunities. The sports book must post lines on hundreds of events every week; those are all opportunities to find the matchups where you are confident that you have an edge. That

---

41 For more on money line bets, see Chapter Nine.

edge, when you think the odds favor you and not the sports book, is what sports bettors refer to as "getting value," or an *overlay*. For example, if after thoughtful analysis you think the Vikings will win the game by 14 points and the point spread is only 10, you have an overlay. In this instance, the odds appear to be in your favor; find enough of those situations and you can make a profit betting on sports.

Why Lines Move: Not All Point Spreads Are Equal

Shopping for the best available line or quote is another way you can boost your Win Rate and make more winning wagers. Every sports book sets its point spreads differently and changes its lines based on circumstances. This difference in pricing between the sports books provides an additional opportunity to add value to the bets you are placing.

Remember that sports books make their money by withholding a commission on winning wagers. So they do have a small vested interest in the outcome of every game. For the sports books, the ideal is a perfectly balanced line where the money taken from the losers goes to the winners, and the house gets to pocket its service charge from all the winners. In the real world, the betting action is rarely perfectly balanced. When wagering action isn't balanced, the sports book is in danger of paying out more than it takes in. This is when the sports book is exposed. Each sports book determines how exposed it can be on any given event. A combination of its own tolerance for risk and the wagering activity is what drives line changes.

If a sports book has $5,500 wagered by its clients on Atlanta -4 and $2,200 wagered on Buffalo +4, then the sports book stands to lose $2,800, assuming Atlanta covers. (The sports book collects $2,200 from players who bet on Buffalo but has to pay $5,000 to players who bet on Atlanta). On the other hand, the sports book can win $3,500 if Buffalo covers (the sports book collects $5,500 from players who bet on Atlanta but has to pay $2,000 to players who bet on Buffalo). This may not seem like much risk, but if you multiply these numbers by 10, 20, 50, 1,000 or more, you can appreciate why sports books move lines to balance action. One sports book might move to -4.5 when it is exposed by $5,000 on Atlanta. Another sports book might be comfortable holding at -4 until it has $25,000 of unbalanced action. It all depends on the anticipated total amount bet, the sport, the game and the sports book's own tolerance for risk.

Some books may shade the line a half point or more in one direction or another to generate more wagering on the team they think will not cover. If they like Atlanta to cover the -4, they might open the line at -4.5. If they like Buffalo, they might open the line at -3.5. Or they may open the game at -4 and simply decide to allow more risk on one team than the other. For example, if the house likes Atlanta and has a normal risk tolerance of $25,000 on a given line, the sports book may then decide to move to -4.5 after only being $10,000 offside on Atlanta, but would wait to be $40,000 offside on Buffalo before moving to -3.5.

Right now, other than cursing me for introducing too much math, you may be thinking, "Why don't sports books just keep moving the line until they are balanced?" Because there is also risk involved every time a line is moved. Here are some very simple examples to demonstrate the risks the sports books face.

Example #1: The betting is $110 on Atlanta -4, so the sports book moves the line to -4.5 to attract wagering action on Buffalo (now at +4.5). Now someone bets on Buffalo +4.5 for $110, so the sports book is happy. However, the book gets dinged if the final score is Atlanta -4, because the player who bet on Atlanta has his wager pushed, but the person who bet on Buffalo wins and collects $100, so the sports book loses $100. When the final score lands on one of the outer extremes of the range of point spreads for a game, the sports book is said to have been "sided."

Example #2: The betting is $110 on Atlanta -3.5, so the sports book moves the line to -4 to attract action on Buffalo. Despite its best efforts, the book still takes $110 more on Atlanta and decides to move to -4.5. Someone finally bets on Buffalo +4.5 for $220, so the sports book is happy; they have $220 total bet on each team. In this case, however, the sports book gets dinged if the final score is Atlanta -4, because the player who bet on Atlanta -3.5 wins $100, the player who bet at -4 has his wager pushed and the player who bet on Buffalo wins and collects $200, so the sports book loses $300. When the final score lands between the outer extremes of the range of point spreads for a game, the sports book is said to have been "middled."

The risk of getting sided or middled keeps sports books from constantly moving lines, and it is the risk of having a position on a losing team that forces them to move the line. Sports books that move lines too far can suffer heavy losses, as will sports books that don't move lines enough. The difficulty in knowing when to move lines is what makes line-making an art and not a science. Just know that every sports book moves its lines a little differently, so every day there are differences in the lines posted between sports books for the exact same game. The differences among the books provide you, the value-seeking bettor, with an opportunity to do some bargain shopping and make your wager at the best price.

Off-Standard Point Spreads

Sports books also use off-standard point spreads to balance the betting on an event. The standard payoff on a football or basketball point spread is 10/11 (or -110), where the bettor must risk $11 to win $10, but occasionally sports books deviate from that. Anything other than -110 is referred to as an "off-standard" line, and it happens a lot in football. The reason is because football is unique among the major pro sports in terms of how points are scored. In baseball, hockey and soccer, all scores are valued as a single point. These sports also tend to have low scores and low margins of victory, so point spreads aren't used in the same way as they are in football and basketball, causing money lines to be the most common form of betting.

Basketball scores come in increments of 1, 2 or 3, but the high amount of scoring makes for an even distribution of final scores. As a result, basketball is perhaps the simplest sport to wager on in terms of lines offered. Football gets complicated because the scoring comes in chunks of 3 and 7 points. There are also other scoring possibilities, with safeties scoring 2 points, missed extra points making a touchdown worth only 6, and the 2-point conversion making 8 a possibility, but they are less likely combinations.

What's more, in football scoring tends to take place an average of only about eight times a game and, as a result of these few scoring occurrences, the final scores do group around certain numbers, known as key numbers. The major key numbers are 3 and 7, but 1, 4, 6, 10, 13 and 14 also have a high likelihood of being the final margin of victory and are sometimes referred to as minor key numbers.

If we look at how all these numbers relate to 3 and 7, it's easy to see why they occur frequently. Table 7.1 shows the frequency of certain final game margins for the NFL, as well as the relationship between the number of points and a combination of touchdowns and field goals:

Table 7.1

Game Margin	Frequency	Combinations
3 points	16.0%	Field Goal
7 points	11.3%	Touchdown
6 points	6.6%	2 Field Goals
10 points	5.1%	Touchdown and Field Goal

Let's use an imaginary Pittsburgh–New England game to illustrate the danger that key numbers pose to sports books, and the actions they must take to avoid suffering significant losses. Say the opening point spread in this case is Pittsburgh -2.5. At -2.5, bettors love the Steelers, but if the sports books move to -3, the action will shift to New England. If 3 weren't a key number this would be no problem, as the sports books would simply move between the two numbers to balance action. But moving between 2.5 and a key number of 3 entails large risks.

In the most basic case, let's assume two wagers on the Pittsburgh–New England game. One wager is at $110 to win $100 on the Steelers -2.5 and the other wager is at $110 to win $100 on the Patriots +3. If the game ended with the Steelers up 3, the sports book would risk being sided. In this instance, the Pittsburgh wager would win but the Patriots wager would push, so the sports book would lose $100.

The chance that a football game will be decided by a difference of 3 points is roughly 16 percent, as shown in Table 7.1. Since there is an even split between the amount wagered on Pittsburgh and the amount wagered on New England, the chance of a 3-point favorite's winning by 3 is about 8 percent. That means 8 percent of such games would result in the sports book's being sided or middle. Over time, this could be disastrous for a business where 4.5 percent is the desired profit margin!

In order to balance wagering activity without moving on or off key numbers, sports books alter the odds associated with the point spread. Remember most point spreads are offered at standard odds of -110, meaning you must risk $110 to win $100. So when sports books move a point spread, the odds don't change, as the spreads only affect whether your wager is a winner or not. Changing the odds, on the other hand, doesn't affect whether your wager is a winner or not, but instead affects the payout. By changing the odds away from the standard of -110, the sports books can make the same point spread more or less attractive to the bettors.

Back to the example, where bettors like the Steelers -2.5 and also like the Patriots +3, a middle ground is the bookmaker's only choice. In this case, the line might be Steelers -2.5 -120 (making the Pats +2.5 even) or Steelers -3 even (making the Pats +3 --120). Bettors now have a choice: They could take Pittsburgh at only -2.5 but would have to risk $120 to win $100, or they could give up the 3 points but risk only $100 to win $100. Or New England bettors could now get +3 instead of +2.5 but would have to risk $120 instead of $100 to win $100. Off-standard lines are used to balance the sports wagering activity without having to move on and off a key number. This practice is far more common in the NFL than most bettors realize. Now, when you see a sports book offer an off-standard point spread, you will understand why and benefit by finding even more value in the quoted odds.

The Battle of the Books: The Internet vs. Las Vegas

Now that you know how point spreads are set and changed, let's look at the different types of sports books and how you can best take advantage of them.

A land-based book is one in which you have to be present in order to place a bet. In the United States, most of the legally licensed, land-based sports books are in Las Vegas. There, bettors stand in line, cash in hand, at sports betting counters waiting to place their wagers with sports book employees. This limits the number of wagers that you can place at any point in time. Conversely, Internet books can process thousands of transactions simultaneously. Since it is not necessary to have a person handle every wager, Internet books have much lower cost structures. These cost advantages are *sometimes* passed along to bettors in the form of lower commission charges.

Las Vegas sports books also suffer some geographical influence. Their clients are predominantly from California, Nevada, Arizona and other nearby states. Many of those clients bet their favorite teams, and the hometown bias tends to drive up the price on West Coast teams. Internet sports books can suffer from the same issue if their marketing is heavy in one city or state, but since comparisons are very easy to do over the Internet, those biases don't last long. Thoughtful players, looking for an edge, move in to take advantage of the values they see in the online point spreads, which in turn causes the Internet line quotes to become more balanced between all the Internet sports books.

Imagine being in Las Vegas and trying to go from the Mirage to Bally's, from Bally's to the Bellagio and then to Mandalay Bay so that you could check the posted lines. It would take hours. By the time you realized the original line at the Mirage was the best, the odds would have probably changed! With your computer, on the other hand, you can check the lines at dozens of Internet sports books in mere seconds. You don't have to drive through traffic, pay for parking (or taxis), walk through the casino maze, and then wait in line to place a wager. With Internet sports books, you can compare lines very quickly and act almost instantly when you see a line you like.

The Internet makes it very easy to get the best odds on any game. Yet while there are a lot of advantages to sports betting online, Las Vegas books will always have a place in the market. Sitting in a comfortable room with hundreds of other sports fans, tracking all the point spreads, watching dozens of TVs, drinking ice cold beer and eating 99-cent hot dogs is just too much fun to be completely replaced by the online experience.

Attention Value Shoppers!

If you have an account at only one sports book, you have no choice but to either accept the line offered or not bet. If you use two sports books, you can compare the lines offered and wager on the one that provides you with the best opportunity to win your bet. In an NFL matchup between Dallas and Washington, why would you wager Dallas at -7.5 if you could have made the same wager on Dallas with another sports book at -7?

Estimates vary, but getting an extra half point can increase your chance of winning a wager by about 4 percent.[42] You can imagine the compounding effect of getting an extra half point or full point on every bet over the course of a full season.

This is particularly important around the key numbers in football, 3 and 7, and smaller point spreads in other sports. In other words, it is more likely that the difference between a 2-point and a 2.5-point line is going to be of more significance than the difference between a 22-point and a 22.5-point line. But it doesn't mean you shouldn't make an effort to get the best line possible every time. As an example, we can look at a college football game between Alabama and Tennessee. There can be times when the lines quoted by various sports books might range from Alabama -9 to -10.5. If Alabama wins by a final score of 16-6, which sports book you chose would make a big difference as to whether you will be cashing a winning ticket or taking a loss.

It's up to you to decide how many sports books you should use. Too few means you probably won't have enough variation in the lines quoted. On the other hand, having too many may cause you to lose some opportunities because it might take too long to shop all the lines and your sports betting capital could be spread too thin. Be sure to choose sports books where it is easy to access the features you need very quickly. The *USA Today* website

---

42 Derived from *Sports Book Management — A Guide for the Legal Bookmaker.*

(www.usatoday.com) provides a side-by-side comparison of the lines quoted by some of the most popular sports books. Any of the sports books on the *USA Today* website would be good additions to your lineup of wagering alternatives. The magic number is probably five sports books. But if you have only one account, just adding another sports book to get one more set of line quotes could make a big difference to your bottom-line profits at the end of the season. A half point can turn a loss into a push or a push into a win. Getting a few extra wins or pushes over the course of the season makes that extra shopping well worth the effort.

Timing Can Add Value

Another factor in beating the point spread and boosting your Win Rate is timing. Sometimes the morning paper says the point spread is Cowboys -8, but by the time you go to bet, the point spread is -9.5.

Paying close attention to opening lines and then monitoring how the point spread moves before placing a bet can add value. For example, if a line opens at -6.5 and moves to -6, you know sports books are getting action on the underdog. If you like the favorite in that particular game, you may be better served by waiting as the point spread moves from -6 to -5.5 to -5 over the course of the day or the week. This is tougher to do than shopping for the best line and takes some experience to get a feel for which way point spreads move. But after a couple of weeks of tracking opening and closing lines, you will be well prepared to get the best possible number on your wagers.

As a starting point, experienced bettors use the following guideline for shopping football point spreads. Generally the public prefers favorites (and so-called *overs* when it comes to total score bets, meaning a bet that the total points scored will be over the amount listed by the sports book), so the lines tend to move in that direction (but not always, or sports books would simply raise their opening lines). Thus the rule of thumb is to play favorites and overs early and underdogs and unders late. You won't get the absolute best point spread every time by following this guideline, but it should serve as a solid base and will boost your Win Rate.

Choose Your Path for Financial Reward

Imagine making money from reading the sports pages, listening to sports talk radio, watching pre-game shows, checking sports websites and passionately viewing dozens of games on television. If you are successful at sports betting, the financial rewards can be greater than you ever dreamed possible. Soon you'll need to decide how to manage your winnings.

As in any financial endeavor, sports wagering involves allocating capital in a disciplined and thoughtful way. When approached in a businesslike manner, betting on sports embodies all the essential values of the free-enterprise system. It rewards hard work, intelligence, research and judgment. When conducted as a profit-making enterprise, sports wagering is a highly sophisticated undertaking that is based on information gathering, statistical analysis and creative insight. And as with any serious investment or business venture, sports wagering involves taking calculated risks when the odds are with you.

Investor or Business Owner?

There are two ways to approach sports wagering in a businesslike fashion. You can view it from the perspective of either a financial investor or a business owner. Both can be extremely rewarding, but there is a difference.

And it is essential that you decide which approach best fits your situation so you can maximize your chances for success.

If you don't need the cash earned from your sports betting activities, it's best to be an investor. Investors have the luxury of achieving the maximum benefit from compound returns. Ben Franklin once said, "Money can beget money, and its offspring can beget more." Compounding is when your money makes money. It's a simple yet effective way to build wealth. There is nothing you have to do (other than make winning bets) to take advantage of compounding. The trick is, you need to leave the money alone and let it grow, which prompted Warren Buffett's longtime partner Charlie Munger to say, "Never interrupt it unnecessarily."

The power of compounding is why investors focus on the accumulation and growth of their money. They think about turning $10,000 into $100,000, or even $1 million, over a period of time. Investors have other sources of income, perhaps a full-time job, or they may already be wealthy. They are not interested in paying themselves from their sports wagering activities. They look at sports wagering and ask, "How much money can I accumulate over a three-year period?" Investors are eyeing the pot of gold at the end of the rainbow.

On the other hand, business owners are interested in supporting themselves from the profits their business generates. They place more emphasis on current cash flow than on accumulated value. They view their business as a source of income to provide more money to spend today. They ask themselves, "How much money can I make this year and how much next year and how much the year after that?" They prefer cash in hand and are less concerned about future values.[43]

---

43 For the overwhelming majority of successful sports bettors, wagering is fun and profitable. But it is important to note that for a *few people,* sports wagering can cross the line from being an entertaining intellectual exercise to becoming an unhealthy compulsion (just like excessive day trading). When the behavior becomes extreme, it needs to be treated like any other addiction — with the help of a professional. It is unlikely that you will ever fall into this category. But it may be a good idea to have an outside adviser who periodically assesses how you are doing and whether you have developed any bad habits. Those bad habits will probably not rise to the level of compulsive gambling and may involve nothing more than adjusting your wagering activities to keep them in line with your actual winnings.

Regardless of which path — investor or business owner — best fits you and your needs, there are some essential requirements to get started. First, you will need a certain amount of sports wagering capital — at least $500, but $1,000 or even $5,000 would be better. Next, you must have a computer (or access to a computer) with a high-speed modem and a Web browser. Spreadsheet software such as Microsoft Excel is also useful. Even if you plan to wager only at Las Vegas sports books, a computer is essential because the Internet will serve as your primary resource to access the information required for your game analysis. Newspapers and sporting magazines will be secondary sources. And as with any research-intensive profession, there are also a number of sport-specific resources to which you will need to subscribe, such as *Phil Steele's College Football Annual* or the *Blue Ribbon College Basketball Yearbook*.

With those few tools you are ready to start, be it as investor or business owner.

Investors Look at the Scorecard

The incredible power of compounded returns is why investors put their capital on the line in the financial markets every day. Applied to sports betting, the concept of compounding goes like this: If you don't spend any of the winnings you make in the first year, the next year you earn money on both your beginning capital and the winnings from the first year. In the third year, you earn money on your beginning capital and the first two years of winnings. You get the picture. The concept of using the money earned from your winning bets to make even more winning bets is the miracle of compounding. It's a snowball effect: As your capital rolls down the hill, it becomes bigger and bigger. Even if you start with a small snowball, given enough time and the sports betting edge provided by *Get In and Win*, you can end up with an extremely large snowball in the end.

Intelligently thought-out investment programs begin with projections of future compound returns. For your sports wagering activities, I developed the Scorecard to help you calculate your estimated compound returns. To complete the Scorecard, you need to know the following:

> ➤ The beginning amount of your sports wagering capital
> ➤ An estimate of your expected Win Rate
> ➤ The number of bets you anticipate making per year

With just these three inputs, you can use the Scorecard to project the amount of money you can expect to have at the end of a three-year period. Taking an investment view, you should be able to make between 20 and 25 bets per week, which over a year approximates about 1,000 bets.[44]

Using the Scorecard, I have prepared three examples of how to calculate the amount of money you can expect to accumulate in three years using the *Get In and Win* System, with beginning capital amounts of $500, $1,000 and $5,000. The capital accumulated as shown on Scorecards 8.1, 8.2 and 8.3 at the end of a three-year period, assuming even modestly successful Win Rates of 60 percent and 65 percent, is really incredible — even for an experienced market professional like me.

Scorecard 8.1

$500 SCORECARD			

Beginning Capital	$500		

Win Rate	60%	Year 1	Year 2	Year 3
Beginning Betting Capital		500	4,000	32,000
Anticipated Wagers Per Year		1,000	1,000	1,000
Expected Win Rate		60%	60%	60%
Wagers Per Week		80	80	80

---

44 See Chapter Six for more about minimum and maximum number of bets and the 5 percent wager size.

Bet Size @ 5%	25	200	1,600
Amount Won Per Bet	23	180	1,440
Amount Lost Per Bet	(25)	(200)	(1,600)
Wins Per Year	600	600	600
Losses Per Year	400	400	400
Money Won	13,500	108,000	864,000
Money Lost	(10,000)	(80,000)	(640,000)
Ending Capital	4,000	32,000	256,000

Win Rate	65%	Year 1	Year 2	Year 3
Beginning Betting Capital		500	6,375	81,281
Anticipated Wagers Per Year		1,000	1,000	1,000
Expected Win Rate		65%	65%	65%
Wagers Per Week		80	80	80
Bet Size @ 5%		25	319	4,064
Amount Won Per Bet		23	287	3,658
Amount Lost Per Bet		(25)	(319)	(4,064)

Wins Per Year	650	650	650
Losses Per Year	350	350	350
Money Won	14,625	186,469	2,377,477
Money Lost	(8,750)	(111,563)	(1,422,422)
Ending Capital	6,375	81,281	1,036,336

Scorecard 8.2

$1,000 SCORECARD

Beginning Capital $1,000

Win Rate 60%	Year 1	Year 2	Year 3
Beginning Betting Capital	1,000	8,000	64,000
Anticipated Wagers Per Year	1,000	1,000	1,000
Expected Win Rate	60%	60%	60%
Wagers Per Week	80	80	80
Bet Size @ 5%	50	400	3,200
Amount Won Per Bet	45	360	2,880
Amount Lost Per Bet	(50)	(400)	(3,200)
Wins Per Year	600	600	600
Losses Per Year	400	400	400

Money Won	27,000	216,000	1,728,000
Money Lost	(20,000)	(160,000)	(1,280,000)
Ending Capital	8,000	64,000	512,000

Win Rate	65%	Year 1	Year 2	Year 3
Beginning Betting Capital		1,000	12,750	162,563
Anticipated Wagers Per Year		1,000	1,000	1,000
Expected Win Rate		65%	65%	65%
Wagers Per Week		80	80	80
Bet Size @ 5%		50	638	8,128
Amount Won Per Bet		45	574	7,315
Amount Lost Per Bet		(50)	(638)	(8,128)
Wins Per Year		650	650	650
Losses Per Year		350	350	350
Money Won		29,250	372,938	4,754,953
Money Lost		(17,500)	(223,125)	(2,844,844)
Ending Capital		12,750	162,563	2,072,672

Scorecard 8.3

$5,000 SCORECARD

Beginning Capital $5,000

Win Rate 60%	Year 1	Year 2	Year 3
Beginning Betting Capital	5,000	40,000	320,000
Anticipated Wagers Per Year	1,000	1,000	1,000
Expected Win Rate	60%	60%	60%
Wagers Per Week	80	80	80
Bet Size @ 5%	250	2,000	16,000
Amount Won Per Bet	225	1,800	14,400
Amount Lost Per Bet	(250)	(2,000)	(16,000)
Wins Per Year	600	600	600
Losses Per Year	400	400	400
Money Won	135,000	1,080,000	8,640,000
Money Lost	(100,000)	(800,000)	(6,400,000)
Ending Capital	40,000	320,000	2,560,000

Win Rate	65%	Year 1	Year 2	Year 3
Beginning Betting Capital		5,000	63,750	812,813
Anticipated Wagers Per Year		1,000	1,000	1,000
Expected Win Rate		65%	65%	65%
Wagers Per Week		80	80	80
Bet Size @ 5%		250	3,188	40,641
Amount Won Per Bet		225	2,869	36,577
Amount Lost Per Bet		(250)	(3,188)	(40,641)
Wins Per Year		650	650	650
Losses Per Year		350	350	350
Money Won		146,250	1,864,688	23,774,766
Money Lost		(87,500)	(1,115,625)	(14,224,219)
Ending Capital		63,750	812,813	10,363,359

When It Seems Too Good to Be True, It Really Is

The ending capital amounts for Year Three on the $1,000 Scorecard for the 65 percent Win Rate (Scorecard 8.2), and for Year Three on the $5,000 Scorecard for both the 60 percent and 65 percent Win Rate (Scorecard 8.3), are more than truly amazing, with payouts over a million dollars in every case. Yet while these amounts are theoretically attainable, it is not likely to occur because sports books often limit bets to $5,000 or less.[45] This is because most sports betting is done for fun, and the individual betting amounts are usually in the $50 to $100 range. Because the sport book's goal is to minimize its risk by having equal amounts bet on both sides of the point spread, accepting oversize bets could leave it heavily exposed to risk. It is much harder to balance a large bet with a number of smaller ones.

More realistic projections of ending capital amounts result by limiting the bet size to $5,000, as shown on Scorecards 8.4 and 8.5:

Scorecard 8.4

$1,000 SCORECARD with limits			
Beginning Capital	$1,000		
Win Rate 60%	Year 1	Year 2	Year 3
Beginning Betting Capital	1,000	8,000	64,000
Anticipated Wagers Per Year	1,000	1,000	1,000
Expected Win Rate	60%	60%	60%
Wagers Per Week	80	80	80
Bet Size @ 5%	50	400	3,200
Amount Won Per Bet	45	360	2,880
Amount Lost Per Bet	(50)	(400)	(3,200)
Wins Per Year	600	600	600

45 It's the bet size limit that keeps serious Wall Street hedge fund investors from applying their skills in the sports betting markets. In the financial markets, there are no such limits. And it is this lack of serious competition from other professional bettors that presents the Intelligent Bettor with an opportunity to earn significant returns.

Losses Per Year	400	400	400
Money Won	27,000	216,000	1,728,000
Money Lost	(20,000)	(160,000)	(1,280,000)
Ending Capital	8,000	64,000	512,000

Win Rate	65%	Year 1	Year 2	Year 3
Beginning Betting Capital		1,000	12,750	162,563
Anticipated Wagers Per Year		1,000	1,000	1,000
Expected Win Rate		65%	65%	65%
Wagers Per Week		80	80	80
Bet Size @ 5%		50	638	5,000
Amount Won Per Bet		45	574	4,500
Amount Lost Per Bet		(50)	(638)	(5,000)
Wins Per Year		650	650	650
Losses Per Year		350	350	350
Money Won		29,250	372,938	2,925,000
Money Lost		(17,500)	(223,125)	(1,750,000)
Ending Capital		12,750	162,563	1,337,563

Scorecard 8.5

$5,000 SCORECARD with limits			

Beginning Capital $5,000

Win Rate 60%	Year 1	Year 2	Year 3
Beginning Betting Capital	5,000	40,000	320,000
Anticipated Wagers Per Year	1,000	1,000	1,000
Expected Win Rate	60%	60%	60%
Wagers Per Week	80	80	80
Bet Size @ 5%	250	2,000	5,000
Amount Won Per Bet	225	1,800	4,500
Amount Lost Per Bet	(250)	(2,000)	(5,000)
Wins Per Year	600	600	600
Losses Per Year	400	400	400
Money Won	135,000	1,080,000	2,700,000
Money Lost	(100,000)	(800,000)	(2,000,000)
Ending Capital	40,000	320,000	1,020,000

Win Rate 65%	Year 1	Year 2	Year 3
Beginning Betting Capital	5,000	63,750	812,813
Anticipated Wagers Per Year	1,000	1,000	1,000
Expected Win Rate	65%	65%	65%
Wagers Per Week	80	80	80
Bet Size @ 5%	250	3,188	5,000
Amount Won Per Bet	225	2,869	4,500
Amount Lost Per Bet	(250)	(3,188)	(5,000)
Wins Per Year	650	650	650
Losses Per Year	350	350	350
Money Won	146,250	1,864,688	2,925,000
Money Lost	(87,500)	(1,115,625)	(1,750,000)
Ending Capital	63,750	812,813	1,987,813

As you can see, even after limiting the individual bet size to $5,000, you can still finish your third year with over a million dollars in profit, having started with just $1,000, if you can achieve a 65 percent Win Rate.

Using these Scorecards as guides, you are now ready to complete your own Scorecard using the blank worksheet at the end of this chapter. As you will soon see when completing our own Scorecard, even modest assumptions produce spectacular long-term returns.[46]

---

46 Keep in mind the $5,000 limit for an individual bet.

Your Own Sports Franchise

Looking at sports wagering as an investment activity is all well and good if you can wait for the money. But in many instances there is a need for cash along the way. For those in need of cash flow, think of your wagering as operating your own sports franchise. But before opening your sports business, you need to ask yourself three basic questions:

1. Do I have the motivation and discipline to do the research required to make smart wagers?
2. Do I have the time available to commit to the enterprise to make it successful?
3. Am I really serious about approaching sports wagering as a cash-generating business versus sitting back on the couch and having fun?

If you answered yes to all three of these questions, you are ready to get started.

How much money do you need to start? You can get going with as little as $1,000, but with that limited amount of capital, building cash flow will be a very slow process. For $5,000 you can be up and running with the opportunity to generate meaningful profits within three months. If you have $7,500 or more to commit, then you are way ahead in your quest for significant financial rewards.

You need to do all the groundwork to ensure success. That means starting with enough money to support yourself until returns start to come in. You need to honestly assess *all* your expenses (especially for relocation if you have to move to someplace where betting is legal) as well as how much you will be betting, and plan for the worst-case returns.

A Plan for Business Success

Starting a successful and long-lasting business means having a carefully thought-out plan. When it comes to the sports betting business, you need to know where you are headed *before you begin* in order to effectively execute your plan. As Yogi Berra said, "If you don't know where you're going, you might not get there." Having a good plan is especially important when faced with the curves in the road that will inevitably come your way. A business plan may sound like a daunting task, but it's not. Business plans are simply guides to taking action.

A business plan is a map for the course of a business over a specific period of time. For your sports wagering franchise, you should have a three-year plan. It should focus in detail on the coming 12 months and deal with the following two years in a more general fashion. Here are two sayings to keep in mind:

"Luck is the residue of design." – Branch Rickey

"Genius is 1 percent inspiration and 99 percent perspiration." – Thomas Edison

Branch Rickey was a sports innovator, the first modern general manager of baseball. He mastered scouting, player acquisition and development, and business affairs. He invented baseball's farm system and put together World Series winners for the St. Louis Cardinals and Brooklyn Dodgers. He also signed Jackie Robinson and was thus responsible for the integration of baseball.

In short, he was no dummy. He knew that so-called good luck was actually the result of a lot of preparation and planning. This is also what Edison meant. Edison knew that all that preparing takes time and hard work. They both understood the Five P's: Proper Planning Prevents Poor Performance.

There is money to be made operating a sports wagering business, but you won't make it overnight. A business plan is the first step.

Cash in Hand Every Three Months

To help you develop a plan for paying yourself, I streamlined the business planning process into a worksheet called the Sports Wagering Cash Flow Plan. It will let you quickly work through the planning process, so you can get to the more exciting part of your business — placing winning sports bets. The plan provides a complete picture of your expected financial results so you know when and how much to pay yourself.

The key question is, "When is it OK to take cash out of my business without hurting my chances for future success?" Using the Rule of Large Numbers (as discussed in Chapter Six), I determined that the appropriate time to assess your operating results and pay yourself is after every 250 wagers. When making 20 bets per week, 250 total wagers happens about every three months, which means paying yourself on a quarterly basis. After every 250 bets, you can determine your cash payout and, at the same time, change your assumed Win Rate or keep it the same. But keep in mind, the amount of your beginning sports betting capital (which is used to determine your individual 5 percent bet size) only resets annually, or after every 1,000 wagers.

The Sports Wagering Cash Flow Plan

The Sports Wagering Cash Flow Plan is a three-year financial projection built around five inputs:

1. Beginning Sports Betting Capital
2. Anticipated Wagers Per Quarter
3. Expected Win Rate
4. Quarterly Operating Expenses[47]
5. Profit Payout Rate[48]

Here's an example to show how the Plan works. The cash flow plan presented in Table 8.6 (at the end of this chapter) assumes $1,000 of beginning sports betting capital, 250 bets per quarter, a Win Rate of 65 percent, Quarterly Operating Expenses of $500 and a Payout Rate of 100 percent. Table 8.6 reports that the quarterly cash profit that you can expect to pay

---

47 Operating expenses include payments for computer hardware and software, Internet service, sports magazines and newsletters and any other out-of-pocket expenses related to your sports betting franchise.

48 The Profit Payout Rate is the percentage of the profits you want to withdraw each quarter. For example, if you want to take all the profits, the profit payout rate is 100 percent. If you want to pay yourself half the profits, the profit payout rate is 50 percent.

yourself is $2,390 quarterly ($9,560 annually), based on the assumptions above for each of the three years. At the end of the three-year period, you have the same $1,000 of sports betting capital available that you started with. Not bad for a $1,000 initial investment that you get back at the end of the third year.

One thing this planning exercise tells you is that spending all your profits from an initial investment of only $1,000 is not going to put you in a Skyloft suite at the MGM Grand. Let's face it — annual cash flow of $9,000 isn't going to change your lifestyle, which is why I recommend investing, not spending, your profits. But it doesn't have to be either/or.

Let's see what happens when you reinvest some of the profit back into your sports wagering business, instead of paying it all out. Table 8.7 (at the end of this chapter) uses the same assumptions as Table 8.6, except that instead of paying out all the profits, a Payout Rate of 75 percent is used. This means that you pay out 75 percent of the profits every quarter and leave the remaining 25 percent to accumulate, so that you can increase the beginning betting capital at the beginning of Year Two and Year Three.

As would be expected, Table 8.7 shows that the quarterly payout to you in Year One decreases to $1,793 quarterly ($7,170 annually). But look what happens in Year Two and Year Three. Because you have decided to reinvest in your franchise, the Beginning Sports Betting Capital increases for Year Two and Year Three so that your quarterly payment increases to $6,973 ($27,891 annually) for Year Two and $27,124 quarterly ($108,497 annually) for Year Three. And it gets even better, because your beginning sports betting capital of $1,000 has increased to $48,853 by the end of Year Three. The $48,853 ending capital is yours also and is in addition to all the quarterly withdrawals you have made over the three-year period.

Table 8.8 (at the end of this chapter) presents the financial results that occur when you drop the Payout Rate to 50 percent and plow 50 percent of the profits back into your franchise. For Year One, quarterly distributions decline to $1,195 ($4,780 annually). But the quarterly distributions for Year Two increase to $8,102 ($32,408 annually), and by Year Three they go to $54,932 ($219,729 annually). In addition to these quarterly distributions at the end of Year Three, you will have accumulated sports betting capital of $257,917, which is money available to you above and beyond the quarterly distributions you have paid yourself. Therefore, it you decide to retire after Year Three, you can take the ending capital and head to the beach with about a quarter of a million dollars in your pocket.

To provide an example of the range of amounts that you could earn, Table 8.9 (below) presents, in summary form, the results of the Sports Wagering Cash Flow Plan for a variety of betting scenarios. Specifically, Table 8.9 shows the Quarterly Cash Payout, the Annual Cash Payout and the Ending Capital for a three-year period for various Beginning Capital Amounts and Payout Rates. Table 8.9 also assumes a Win Rate of 65 percent, 250 wagers per quarter (20 bets per week), a 5 percent bet size and $500 of Quarterly Operating Expenses. The 5 percent bet size is reset at the beginning of Years Two and Three, based on the amount of sports betting capital accumulated at that time.

Table 8.9

Beginning Capital	$500		
Quarterly Cash Payout	Year 1	Year 2	Year 3
100% Pay Out	945	945	945
75% Pay Out	709	2,757	10,725
50% Pay Out	473	3,204	21,720
Annual Cash Payout	Year 1	Year 2	Year 3
100% Pay Out	3,780	3,780	3,780
75% Pay Out	2,385	11,028	42,900
50% Pay Out	1,890	12,814	86,880

Ending Capital	Year 1	Year 2	Year 3
100% Pay Out	500	500	500
75% Pay Out	1,445	3,676	19,421
50% Pay Out	2,390	15,204	102,084

Beginning Capital **$1,000**

Quarterly Cash Payout	Year 1	Year 2	Year 3
100% Pay Out	2,390	2,390	2,390
75% Pay Out	1,793	6,973	27,124
50% Pay Out	1,195	8,102	54,932

Annual Cash Payout	Year 1	Year 2	Year 3
100% Pay Out	9,560	9,560	9,560
75% Pay Out	7,170	27,891	108,497
50% Pay Out	4,780	32,408	219,729

Ending Capital	Year 1	Year 2	Year 3
100% Pay Out	1,000	1,000	1,000
75% Pay Out	3,390	12,687	48,853
50% Pay Out	5,780	38,188	257,917

Beginning Capital **$5,000**

Quarterly Cash Payout	Year 1	Year 2	Year 3
100% Pay Out	13,950	13,950	13,950
75% Pay Out	10,463	40,699	158,320
50% Pay Out	6,975	47,291	320,630

Annual Cash Payout	Year 1	Year 2	Year 3
100% Pay Out	55,800	55,800	55,800
75% Pay Out	41,850	162,797	633,278
50% Pay Out	27,900	189,162	577,000*

Ending Capital	Year 1	Year 2	Year 3
100% Pay Out	5,000	5,000	5,000
75% Pay Out	18,950	73,216	284,308
50% Pay Out	32,900	222,062	799,062*

* After applying the $5,000 bet limit.

If you can't see yourself living on the $9,000 a year that starting with $1,000 in capital and a 100 percent Payout Rate would provide, don't worry. The amounts in Tables 8.6 – 8.9 were chosen to make it easy to understand the possible returns that can be earned.

Tables 8.10 and 8.11 (at the end of this chapter) show what your quarterly and annual payouts would be with $7,500 and $10,000 starting stakes and a 100 percent Payout Rate. Table 8.10 reports that you can earn $21,175 every quarter ($84,700 annually) with beginning capital of $7,500, assuming a Win Rate of 65 percent. Table 8.11 shows that you can earn $28,400 every quarter ($113,600 annually) with beginning capital of $10,000, assuming a Win Rate of 65 percent.

As the results from the Sports Wagering Cash Flow Plan presented in these tables demonstrate, there is significant cash flow to be earned from your sports wagering franchise, but it only occurs for those who have the discipline, intelligence and conviction to execute their business plan at the highest level. Your specific results will reflect your individual efforts and sports betting acumen.

When you put together your own Sports Wagering Cash Flow Plan (using the worksheets presented in this chapter as examples), prepare your plan using various assumptions so that you can develop a base-case, a best-case and a worst-case scenario. [49] Your plan should also be dynamic — meaning you should compare your actual results to your original projections and make changes to your cash flow forecast as you gain more experience.

Table 8.6 (Page 1 of 3)

SPORTS WAGERING CASH FLOW PLAN

$1,000 Beginning Capital

100% Payout Rate

Year 1	Quarter 1	Quarter 2	Quarter 3	Quarter 4	Total
Beginning Betting Capital	1,000	1,000	1,000	1,000	
Anticipated Wagers Per Quarter	250	250	250	250	1,000
Expected Win Rate	65%	65%	65%	65%	
Operating Expenses	500	500	500	500	
Wagers Per Week	20	20	20	20	
Bet Size @ 5%	50	50	50	50	
Amount Won per Bet	45	45	45	45	
Amount Lost per Bet	(50)	(50)	(50)	(50)	
Wins Per Quarter	162	162	162	162	648
Losses Per Quarter	88	88	88	88	352
Money Won	7,290	7,290	7,290	7,290	29,160
Money Lost	(4,400)	(4,400)	(4,400)	(4,400)	(17,600)

49 Base-case represents the expected results under normal conditions. Best-case represents the expected results when everything goes perfectly. Worst-case shows what happen when everything goes wrong.

Gross Quarterly Profit	2,890	2,890	2,890	2,890	11,560
Operating Expenses	(500)	(500)	(500)	(500)	(2,000)
Cash Available for Payout	2,390	2,390	2,390	2,390	9,560
Cash Paid Out	(2,390)	(2,390)	(2,390)	(2,390)	(9,560)
Profit to Reinvest	0	0	0	0	0
Beginning Sports Betting Capital	1,000	1,000	1,000	1,000	
Reinvested Profit	0	0	0	0	
Beginning Capital For Next Quarter	1,000	1,000	1,000	1,000	

Table 8.6 (Page 2 of 3)

SPORTS WAGERING CASH FLOW PLAN

$1,000 Beginning Capital

100% Payout Rate

Year 2	Quarter 1	Quarter 2	Quarter 3	Quarter 4	Total
Beginning Betting Capital	1,000	1,000	1,000	1,000	
Anticipated Wagers Per Quarter	250	250	250	250	1,000
Expected Win Rate	65%	65%	65%	65%	
Operating Expenses	500	500	500	500	
Wagers Per Week	20	20	20	20	
Bet Size @ 5%	50	50	50	50	
Amount Won per Bet	45	45	45	45	
Amount Lost per Bet	(50)	(50)	(50)	(50)	

Wins Per Quarter	162	162	162	162	648
Losses Per Quarter	88	88	88	88	352
Money Won	7,290	7,290	7,290	7,290	29,160
Money Lost	(4,400)	(4,400)	(4,400)	(4,400)	(17,600)
Gross Quarterly Profit	2,890	2,890	2,890	2,890	11,560
Operating Expenses	(500)	(500)	(500)	(500)	(2,000)
Cash Available for Payout	2,390	2,390	2,390	2,390	9,560
Cash Paid Out	(2,390)	(2,390)	(2,390)	(2,390)	(9,560)
Profit to Reinvest	0	0	0	0	0
Beginning Sports Betting Capital	1,000	1,000	1,000	1,000	
Reinvested Profit	0	0	0	0	
Beginning Capital For Next Quarter	1,000	1,000	1,000	1,000	

Table 8.6 (Page 3 of 3)

SPORTS WAGERING CASH FLOW PLAN

$1,000 Beginning Capital

100% Payout Rate

Year 3	Quarter 1	Quarter 2	Quarter 3	Quarter 4	Total
Beginning Betting Capital	1,000	1,000	1,000	1,000	
Anticipated Wagers Per Quarter	250	250	250	250	1,000
Expected Win Rate	65%	65%	65%	65%	
Operating Expenses	500	500	500	500	

Wagers Per Week	20	20	20	20	
Bet Size @ 5%	50	50	50	50	
Amount Won per Bet	45	45	45	45	
Amount Lost per Bet	(50)	(50)	(50)	(50)	
Wins Per Quarter	162	162	162	162	648
Losses Per Quarter	88	88	88	88	352
Money Won	7,290	7,290	7,290	7,290	29,160
Money Lost	(4,400)	(4,400)	(4,400)	(4,400)	(17,600)
Gross Quarterly Profit	2,890	2,890	2,890	2,890	11,560
Operating Expenses	(500)	(500)	(500)	(500)	(2,000)
Cash Available for Payout	2,390	2,390	2,390	2,390	9,560
Cash Paid Out	(2,390)	(2,390)	(2,390)	(2,390)	(9,560)
Profit to Reinvest	0	0	0	0	0
Beginning Sports Betting Capital	1,000	1,000	1,000	1,000	
Reinvested Profit	0	0	0	0	
Beginning Capital For Next Quarter	1,000	1,000	1,000	1,000	

Table 8.7 (Page 1 of 3)

SPORTS WAGERING CASH FLOW PLAN

$1,000 Beginning Capital

75% Payout Rate

Year 1	Quarter 1	Quarter 2	Quarter 3	Quarter 4	Total
Beginning Betting Capital	1,000	1,598	2,195	2,793	

Anticipated Wagers Per Quarter	250	250	250	250	1,000
Expected Win Rate	65%	65%	65%	65%	
Operating Expenses	500	500	500	500	
Wagers Per Week	20	20	20	20	
Bet Size @ 5%	50	50	50	50	
Amount Won per Bet	45	45	45	45	
Amount Lost per Bet	(50)	(50)	(50)	(50)	
Wins Per Quarter	162	162	162	162	648
Losses Per Quarter	88	88	88	88	352
Money Won	7,290	7,290	7,290	7,290	29,160
Money Lost	(4,400)	(4,400)	(4,400)	(4,400)	(17,600)
Gross Quarterly Profit	2,890	2,890	2,890	2,890	11,560
Operating Expenses	(500)	(500)	(500)	(500)	(2,000)
Cash Available for Payout	2,390	2,390	2,390	2,390	9,560
Cash Paid Out	(1,793)	(1,793)	(1,793)	(1,793)	(7,170)
Profit to Reinvest	598	598	598	598	2,390
Beginning Sports Betting Capital	1,000	1,598	2,195	2,793	
Reinvested Profit	598	598	598	598	
Beginning Capital For Next Quarter	1,598	2,195	2,793	3,390	

Table 8.7 (Page 2 of 3)

SPORTS WAGERING CASH FLOW PLAN

$1,000 Beginning Capital

75% Payout Rate

Year 2	Quarter 1	Quarter 2	Quarter 3	Quarter 4	Total
Beginning Betting Capital	3,390	5,714	8,039	10,363	
Anticipated Wagers Per Quarter	250	250	250	250	1,000
Expected Win Rate	65%	65%	65%	65%	
Operating Expenses	500	500	500	500	
Wagers Per Week	20	20	20	20	
Bet Size @ 5%	170	170	170	170	
Amount Won per Bet	153	153	153	153	
Amount Lost per Bet	(170)	(170)	(170)	(170)	
Wins Per Quarter	162	162	162	162	648
Losses Per Quarter	88	88	88	88	352
Money Won	24,713	24,713	24,713	24,713	98,852
Money Lost	(14,916)	(14,916)	(14,916)	(14,916)	(59,664)
Gross Quarterly Profit	9,797	9,797	9,797	9,797	39,188
Operating Expenses	(500)	(500)	(500)	(500)	(2,000)
Cash Available for Payout	9,297	9,297	9,297	9,297	37,188
Cash Paid Out	(6,973)	(6,973)	(6,973)	(6,973)	(27,891)
Profit to Reinvest	2,324	2,324	2,324	2,324	9,297

Beginning Sports Betting Capital	3,390	5,714	8,039	10,363
Reinvested Profit	2,324	2,324	2,324	2,324
Beginning Capital For Next Quarter	5,714	8,039	10,363	12,687

Table 8.7 (Page 3 of 3)

SPORTS WAGERING CASH FLOW PLAN

$1,000 Beginning Capital

75% Payout Rate

Year 3	Quarter 1	Quarter 2	Quarter 3	Quarter 4	Total
Beginning Betting Capital	12,687	21,729	30,770	39,811	
Anticipated Wagers Per Quarter	250	250	250	250	1,000
Expected Win Rate	65%	65%	65%	65%	
Operating Expenses	500	500	500	500	
Wagers Per Week	20	20	20	20	
Bet Size @ 5%	634	634	634	634	
Amount Won per Bet	571	571	571	571	
Amount Lost per Bet	(634)	(634)	(634)	(634)	
Wins Per Quarter	162	162	162	162	648
Losses Per Quarter	88	88	88	88	352
Money Won	92,489	92,489	92,489	92,489	369,956
Money Lost	(55,823)	(55,823)	(55,823)	(55,823)	(223,293)
Gross Quarterly Profit	36,666	36,666	36,666	36,666	146,663
Operating Expenses	(500)	(500)	(500)	(500)	(2,000)

Cash Available for Payout	36,166	36,166	36,166	36,166	144,663
Cash Paid Out	(27,124)	(27,124)	(27,124)	(27,124)	(108,497)
Profit to Reinvest	9,041	9,041	9,041	9,041	36,166
Beginning Sports Betting Capital	12,687	21,729	30,770	39,811	
Reinvested Profit	9,041	9,041	9,041	9,041	
Beginning Capital For Next Quarter	21,729	30,770	39,811	48,853	

Table 8.8 (Page 1 of 3)

SPORTS WAGERING CASH FLOW PLAN

$1,000 Beginning Capital

50% Payout Rate

Year 1	Quarter 1	Quarter 2	Quarter 3	Quarter 4	Total
Beginning Betting Capital	1,000	2,195	3,390	4,585	
Anticipated Wagers Per Quarter	250	250	250	250	1,000
Expected Win Rate	65%	65%	65%	65%	
Operating Expenses	500	500	500	500	
Wagers Per Week	20	20	20	20	
Bet Size @ 5%	50	50	50	50	
Amount Won per Bet	45	45	45	45	
Amount Lost per Bet	(50)	(50)	(50)	(50)	
Wins Per Quarter	162	162	162	162	648
Losses Per Quarter	88	88	88	88	352
Money Won	7,290	7,290	7,290	7,290	29,160
Money Lost	(4,400)	(4,400)	(4,400)	(4,400)	(17,600)

Gross Quarterly Profit	2,890	2,890	2,890	2,890	11,560
Operating Expenses	(500)	(500)	(500)	(500)	(2,000)
Cash Available for Payout	2,390	2,390	2,390	2,390	9,560
Cash Paid Out	(1,195)	(1,195)	(1,195)	(1,195)	(4,780)
Profit to Reinvest	1,195	1,195	1,195	1,195	4,780
Beginning Sports Betting Capital	1,000	2,195	3,390	4,585	
Reinvested Profit	1,195	1,195	1,195	1,195	
Beginning Capital For Next Quarter	2,195	3,390	4,585	5,780	

Table 8.8 (Page 2 of 3)

SPORTS WAGERING CASH FLOW PLAN

$1,000 Beginning Capital

50% Payout Rate

Year 2	Quarter 1	Quarter 2	Quarter 3	Quarter 4	Total
Beginning Betting Capital	5,780	13,882	21,984	30,086	
Anticipated Wagers Per Quarter	250	250	250	250	1,000
Expected Win Rate	65%	65%	65%	65%	
Operating Expenses	500	500	500	500	
Wagers Per Week	20	20	20	20	
Bet Size @ 5%	289	289	289	289	
Amount Won per Bet	260	260	260	260	
Amount Lost per Bet	(289)	(289)	(289)	(289)	
Wins Per Quarter	162	162	162	162	648
Losses Per Quarter	88	88	88	88	352

Money Won	42,136	42,136	42,136	42,136	**168,545**
Money Lost	(25,432)	(25,432)	(25,432)	(25,432)	**(101,728)**
Gross Quarterly Profit	16,704	16,704	16,704	16,704	**66,817**
Operating Expenses	(500)	(500)	(500)	(500)	**(2,000)**
Cash Available for Payout	16,204	16,204	16,204	16,204	**64,817**
Cash Paid Out	(8,102)	(8,102)	(8,102)	(8,102)	**(32,408)**
Profit to Reinvest	8,102	8,102	8,102	8,102	**32,408**
Beginning Sports Betting Capital	5,780	13,882	21,984	30,086	
Reinvested Profit	8,102	8,102	8,102	8,102	
Beginning Capital For Next Quarter	13,882	21,984	30,086	38,188	

Table 8.8 (Page 3 of 3)

SPORTS WAGERING CASH FLOW PLAN

$1,000 Beginning Capital

50% Payout Rate

Year 3	Quarter 1	Quarter 2	Quarter 3	Quarter 4	Total
Beginning Betting Capital	38,188	93,121	148,053	202,985	
Anticipated Wagers Per Quarter	250	250	250	250	1,000
Expected Win Rate	65%	65%	65%	65%	
Operating Expenses	500	500	500	500	
Wagers Per Week	20	20	20	20	
Bet Size @ 5%	1,909	1,909	1,909	1,909	
Amount Won per Bet	1,718	1,718	1,718	1,718	
Amount Lost per Bet	(1,909)	(1,909)	(1,909)	(1,909)	

Wins Per Quarter	162	162	162	162	**648**
Losses Per Quarter	88	88	88	88	**352**
Money Won	278,393	278,393	278,393	278,393	**1,113,574**
Money Lost	(168,029)	(168,029)	(168,029)	(168,029)	**(672,116)**
Gross Quarterly Profit	110,364	110,364	110,364	110,364	**441,458**
Operating Expenses	(500)	(500)	(500)	(500)	**(2,000)**
Cash Available for Payout	109,864	109,864	109,864	109,864	**439,458**
Cash Paid Out	**(54,932)**	**(54,932)**	**(54,932)**	**(54,932)**	**(219,729)**
Profit to Reinvest	54,932	54,932	54,932	54,932	**219,729**
Beginning Sports Betting Capital	38,188	93,121	148,053	202,985	
Reinvested Profit	54,932	54,932	54,932	54,932	
Beginning Capital For Next Quarter	93,121	148,053	202,985	257,917	

Table 8.10 (Page 1 of 3)

SPORTS WAGERING CASH FLOW PLAN

$7,500 Beginning Capital

100% Payout Rate

Year 1	Quarter 1	Quarter 2	Quarter 3	Quarter 4	**Total**
Beginning Betting Capital	7,500	7,500	7,500	7,500	
Anticipated Wagers Per Quarter	250	250	250	250	**1,000**
Expected Win Rate	65%	65%	65%	65%	
Operating Expenses	500	500	500	500	
Wagers Per Week	20	20	20	20	
Bet Size @ 5%	375	375	375	375	

Amount Won per Bet	338	338	338	338	
Amount Lost per Bet	(375)	(375)	(375)	(375)	
Wins Per Quarter	162	162	162	162	648
Losses Per Quarter	88	88	88	88	352
Money Won	54,675	54,675	54,675	54,675	218,700
Money Lost	(33,000)	(33,000)	(33,000)	(33,000)	(132,000)
Gross Quarterly Profit	21,675	21,675	21,675	21,675	86,700
Operating Expenses	(500)	(500)	(500)	(500)	(2,000)
Cash Available for Payout	21,175	21,175	21,175	21,175	84,700
Cash Paid Out	(21,175)	(21,175)	(21,175)	(21,175)	(84,700)
Profit to Reinvest	0	0	0	0	0
Beginning Sports Betting Capital	7,500	7,500	7,500	7,500	
Reinvested Profit	0	0	0	0	
Beginning Capital For Next Quarter	7,500	7,500	7,500	7,500	

Table 8.10 (Page 2 of 3)

SPORTS WAGERING CASH FLOW PLAN

$7,500 Beginning Capital

100% Payout Rate

Year 2	Quarter 1	Quarter 2	Quarter 3	Quarter 4	Total
Beginning Betting Capital	7,500	7,500	7,500	7,500	
Anticipated Wagers Per Quarter	250	250	250	250	1,000
Expected Win Rate	65%	65%	65%	65%	
Operating Expenses	500	500	500	500	

Wagers Per Week	20	20	20	20	
Bet Size @ 5%	375	375	375	375	
Amount Won per Bet	338	338	338	338	
Amount Lost per Bet	(375)	(375)	(375)	(375)	
Wins Per Quarter	162	162	162	162	648
Losses Per Quarter	88	88	88	88	352
Money Won	54,675	54,675	54,675	54,675	218,700
Money Lost	(33,000)	(33,000)	(33,000)	(33,000)	(132,000)
Gross Quarterly Profit	21,675	21,675	21,675	21,675	86,700
Operating Expenses	(500)	(500)	(500)	(500)	(2,000)
Cash Available for Payout	21,175	21,175	21,175	21,175	84,700
Cash Paid Out	(21,175)	(21,175)	(21,175)	(21,175)	(84,700)
Profit to Reinvest	0	0	0	0	0
Beginning Sports Betting Capital	7,500	7,500	7,500	7,500	
Reinvested Profit	0	0	0	0	
Beginning Capital For Next Quarter	7,500	7,500	7,500	7,500	

Table 8.10 (Page 3 of 3)

SPORTS WAGERING CASH FLOW PLAN

$7,500 Beginning Capital

100% Payout Rate

Year 3	Quarter 1	Quarter 2	Quarter 3	Quarter 4	Total
Beginning Betting Capital	7,500	7,500	7,500	7,500	
Anticipated Wagers Per Quarter	250	250	250	250	1,000

Expected Win Rate	65%	65%	65%	65%	
Operating Expenses	500	500	500	500	
Wagers Per Week	20	20	20	20	
Bet Size @ 5%	375	375	375	375	
Amount Won per Bet	338	338	338	338	
Amount Lost per Bet	(375)	(375)	(375)	(375)	
Wins Per Quarter	162	162	162	162	**648**
Losses Per Quarter	88	88	88	88	**352**
Money Won	54,675	54,675	54,675	54,675	**218,700**
Money Lost	(33,000)	(33,000)	(33,000)	(33,000)	**(132,000)**
Gross Quarterly Profit	21,675	21,675	21,675	21,675	**86,700**
Operating Expenses	(500)	(500)	(500)	(500)	**(2,000)**
Cash Available for Payout	21,175	21,175	21,175	21,175	**84,700**
Cash Paid Out	(21,175)	(21,175)	(21,175)	(21,175)	**(84,700)**
Profit to Reinvest	0	0	0	0	0
Beginning Sports Betting Capital	7,500	7,500	7,500	7,500	
Reinvested Profit	0	0	0	0	
Beginning Capital For Next Quarter	7,500	7,500	7,500	7,500	

Table 8.11 (Page 1 of 3)

SPORTS WAGERING CASH FLOW PLAN

$10,000 Beginning Capital

100% Payout Rate

Year 1	Quarter 1	Quarter 2	Quarter 3	Quarter 4	Total
Beginning Betting Capital	10,000	10,000	10,000	10,000	
Anticipated Wagers Per Quarter	250	250	250	250	1,000
Expected Win Rate	65%	65%	65%	65%	
Operating Expenses	500	500	500	500	
Wagers Per Week	20	20	20	20	
Bet Size @ 5%	500	500	500	500	
Amount Won per Bet	450	450	450	450	
Amount Lost per Bet	(500)	(500)	(500)	(500)	
Wins Per Quarter	162	162	162	162	648
Losses Per Quarter	88	88	88	88	352
Money Won	72,900	72,900	72,900	72,900	291,600
Money Lost	(44,000)	(44,000)	(44,000)	(44,000)	(176,000)
Gross Quarterly Profit	28,900	28,900	28,900	28,900	115,600
Operating Expenses	(500)	(500)	(500)	(500)	(2,000)
Cash Available for Payout	28,400	28,400	28,400	28,400	113,600
Cash Paid Out	(28,400)	(28,400)	(28,400)	(28,400)	(113,600)
Profit to Reinvest	0	0	0	0	0
Beginning Sports Betting Capital	10,000	10,000	10,000	10,000	
Reinvested Profit	0	0	0	0	
Beginning Capital For Next Quarter	10,000	10,000	10,000	10,000	

Table 8.11 (Page 2 of 3)

SPORTS WAGERING CASH FLOW PLAN

$10,000 Beginning Capital

100% Payout Rate

Year 2	Quarter 1	Quarter 2	Quarter 3	Quarter 4	Total
Beginning Betting Capital	10,000	10,000	10,000	10,000	
Anticipated Wagers Per Quarter	250	250	250	250	1,000
Expected Win Rate	65%	65%	65%	65%	
Operating Expenses	500	500	500	500	
Wagers Per Week	20	20	20	20	
Bet Size @ 5%	500	500	500	500	
Amount Won per Bet	450	450	450	450	
Amount Lost per Bet	(500)	(500)	(500)	(500)	
Wins Per Quarter	162	162	162	162	648
Losses Per Quarter	88	88	88	88	352
Money Won	72,900	72,900	72,900	72,900	291,600
Money Lost	(44,000)	(44,000)	(44,000)	(44,000)	(176,000)
Gross Quarterly Profit	28,900	28,900	28,900	28,900	115,600
Operating Expenses	(500)	(500)	(500)	(500)	(2,000)
Cash Available for Payout	28,400	28,400	28,400	28,400	113,600
Cash Paid Out	(28,400)	(28,400)	(28,400)	(28,400)	(113,600)
Profit to Reinvest	0	0	0	0	0

Beginning Sports Betting Capital	10,000	10,000	10,000	10,000
Reinvested Profit	0	0	0	0
Beginning Capital For Next Quarter	10,000	10,000	10,000	10,000

Table 8.11 (Page 3 of 3)

SPORTS WAGERING CASH FLOW PLAN

$10,000 Beginning Capital

100% Payout Rate

Year 3	Quarter 1	Quarter 2	Quarter 3	Quarter 4	Total
Beginning Betting Capital	10,000	10,000	10,000	10,000	
Anticipated Wagers Per Qtr	250	250	250	250	1,000
Expected Win Rate	65%	65%	65%	65%	
Operating Expenses	500	500	500	500	
Wagers Per Week	20	20	20	20	
Bet Size @ 5%	500	500	500	500	
Amount Won per Bet	450	450	450	450	
Amount Lost per Bet	(500)	(500)	(500)	(500)	
Wins Per Quarter	162	162	162	162	648
Losses Per Quarter	88	88	88	88	352
Money Won	72,900	72,900	72,900	72,900	291,600
Money Lost	(44,000)	(44,000)	(44,000)	(44,000)	(176,000)
Gross Quarterly Profit	28,900	28,900	28,900	28,900	115,600
Operating Expenses	(500)	(500)	(500)	(500)	(2,000)

Cash Available for Payout	28,400	28,400	28,400	28,400	113,600
Cash Paid Out	(28,400)	(28,400)	(28,400)	(28,400)	(113,600)
Profit to Reinvest	0	0	0	0	0
Beginning Betting Capital	10,000	10,000	10,000	10,000	
Reinvested Profit	0	0	0	0	
Beginning Capital For Next Quarter	10,000	10,000	10,000	10,000	

Hidden Treasures

Proposition Bets: Win or Lose, a Win-Win Situation

Most sports books provide bettors with an opportunity to make bets that are not directly related to the outcome of a game. These bets are known as proposition wagers, commonly called props or prop bets. Prop bets are based on the odds associated with how many times a particular event — sacks, assists or strikeouts, for example — will occur during a game. If you are involved in fantasy sports, many prop bets offer a way to profit on the research you are already doing for your fantasy team. Fantasy players do so much research on individual players that being able to wager on individual players holds a lot of appeal.

Prop bets are usually determined individually by each sports book, so they will not always be the same from one book to the next. While all props are unique among sports books, once you begin analyzing them you will find that each book consistently offers many of the same prop bets week after week to its own customers as a way to keep them coming back. Because most books usually release dozens of props every day, there is a good chance you will find some that provide solid betting value.

The most popular event for sports books in terms of props is the Super Bowl. While there are hundreds of props for the Super Bowl, many of them are too frivolous for the serious bettor. But prop bets are also offered throughout the rest of the football season, and for basketball and baseball too. Typical football prop bets include total passing yards by a quarterback, total number of sacks by one or both teams, rushing yards by a particular player, number of field goals by a kicker, and catches by a receiver.

The following is an example of a common proposition wager:

Thunder vs. Mavericks — 2011 Western Conference Finals
Jason Kidd — Assists in Game 1

Must play in Game 1 of the series for action.

Over	8	(-105)o
Under	8	(-120)u

In the example above, the (-105)o means a $105 bet on Jason Kidd dealing out more than eight assists (the *o* is for *over*) would win $100, if Jason Kidd has nine assists or more in the first game of the series. On the other hand (-120)u means the bettor must risk $125 to win $100 if Kidd has seven or fewer assists (the *u* is for *under*) in Game One. If he has exactly eight assists, then the wager is a push and the bettor gets his money back. Moreover, for the bet to be valid, Kidd must actually play in the game. If he does not play, the bettor's money is also returned, just like a push.

There are four steps to deciding if a proposition bet is worth taking:

> **Step 1:** Determine the *Required Win Percent* for a bet to break even at the odds presented:

Required Win Percent = Amount Risked ÷ (Amount Risked + Amount of Win)

For the line in our example:

> ➤ A line of -105 implies a risk of $105 to win $100. So the Required Win Percent is 51.22 percent [105 ÷ (105 + 100) = 51.22.]
> ➤ A line of -120 implies a risk of $120 to win $100. So the Required Win Percent is 54.55 percent. [120 ÷ (120 + 100) = 54.55]

> **Step 2:** Analyze data from previous games to see the historical record of this event. Based on that, use your judgment to estimate the likelihood of the proposition taking place — in this case the number of assists Jason Kidd will have.

Step 3: Apply what is known as the Poisson distribution to calculate how likely you are to win, depending on which side of the prop bet you take.

The Poisson distribution is the work of an early-19th-century mathematician named Simeon Denis Poisson. It lets you transform your calculations from an informed guesstimate into a statistically valid projection. Suppose you decide the number of assists will be 10. By applying the Poisson distribution, you will know how likely it is that the number of assists will be either more than eight or under eight (the amount asked for in the prop bet). In this case, the Poisson distribution calculations show that 68 percent of the time, Kidd will have eight or more assists in this game, and 32 percent of the time, he will have fewer than eight assists.

The old-fashioned way of solving Poisson distribution problems is to take out a statistics textbook, open it to the Poisson probabilities in the appendix, find the factors and calculate the probabilities. That's easy to do if you happen to have a statistics book at hand, and are confident you can use the tables correctly. But I have made it simpler for you. In the Specialty Plays Playbook you'll find step-by-step instructions and easy-to-use worksheets to calculate the Poisson probabilities for the most popular prop bets for each sport.

Step 4: Compare the Required Win Percent to the Poisson distribution to determine which side of the prop bet offers best value. Since the Poisson probability that Jason Kidd will have more than eight assists is 68 percent, which is greater than the 51.22 percent Required Win Percent, the over bet is the way to go in this instance. In the actual game, Kidd recorded only six assists, so the statistically correct bet would have been a losing wager — demonstrating that betting losses will happen even when your analysis is spot-on. Don't get discouraged when this happens. Recall from Chapter Two that a good process consistently applied will produce winning results, and bear in mind that the rewards from sports betting are earned over time, not overnight.

Unfortunately, the Poisson distribution cannot be used for all prop bets. There are two requirements for it to be applicable: First, the event must be something that is counted one at a time. Second, the expected number of occurrences must be proportional to the length of the event measured. Some events that follow a Poisson distribution are:

➢ The number of hits or strikeouts that occur in a baseball game by an individual player or a team.
➢ The number of 3-pointers, 2-point field goals or free throws made by a player or team in a basketball game.
➢ The number of sacks, field goals or receptions by a player or team in a football game.

By contrast, in football, rushing yards, passing yards and points scored do not follow a Poisson distribution because yards occur in bunches instead of being measured one at a time, and each score is worth more than one point. The same goes for points scored in basketball, because a regular field goal is worth 2 points and a shot from behind the arc is worth 3 points. And since a single hit in baseball can result in multiple runs, runs scored do not follow a Poisson distribution.

Take the time to investigate the props. I call the ones that follow the Poisson distribution Poisson Props, and they provide excellent wagering opportunities.

Betting on Totals: A Simple Path to Success

There is no simpler wager to understand than the game total. Simply add the score of the two teams together, and if it is higher than the posted total, the *over* wins. If it is lower than the posted number, the *under* wins. It doesn't get easier than that. However, many bettors have difficulty predicting outcomes for totals. But you, as an Intelligent Bettor, using the Score Sheets for the NFL and NBA presented in Chapter Five, can actually forecast the total points each team will score in a game. Here's the key:

With totals, you don't need to worry about which team is better. All you need to know is how *the game will be played.*

➢ For football: Is this going to be a game with a lot of passing and lots of plays, or is this going to be a big running game with fewer plays?

> ➤ For basketball: Is it going to be a defensive battle, where each possession is fiercely contested, or is it going to be a run-and-gun, high-scoring affair?

When wagering on totals for football, always be sure to check the weather for any total you bet. Sports books take weather into account and so should you. Rain and snow aren't as important factors as many people make them out to be, since defenders are just as likely to slip as offensive players and one or two big plays can drive a total way up. Wind, on the other hand, is underrated (in my opinion) and forces teams to run more. This can eat up the clock and help lower total scores. With basketball, pay attention to the game tempo because the pace of the game determines whether it will be a grind-it-out, low-scoring contest or a freewheeling, high-scoring game.

Totals are a very important part of a bettor's arsenal. Spend time looking through the totals of all the games and you can find some betting opportunities.

Money Lines: It's Not as Hard as You Think

Most bettors favor point spreads over money lines, simply because point spreads are easier to understand. With point spreads, it's easy to spot the difference between -3 and -4, right? But how much value is there between money lines of -170 and -210? Most people don't get that; it's just not intuitive to most bettors. Bettors like point spreads because there isn't a lot of math involved and they seem less intimidating. However, the math for the money line is actually much easier than most people realize.

Here is a quick primer:

To start with, reading a money line is very simple. A typical money line would look something like this:

Denver Broncos -160, Miami Dolphins +140. The -160 means you must risk $160 to win $100 on the Broncos while the +140 means you get back $140 for each $100 risked should the Dolphins win outright.

Any minus number means the amount that is put at risk to win $100, and any plus number is the payoff for risking $100. It's that simple. In the event of a tie, all money line wagers are settled as a push, and bets are refunded.

The difference between the two lines is described in "cents." In football, it typically starts at 20 cents and gets larger as the numbers get higher. For example, if the favorite is -240, the underdog may be +200, a difference of 40 cents. The higher difference at higher numbers simply serves to keep the commission for the sports book roughly the same as a percentage of the amount wagered.

Thus there is a question you need to ask yourself about every single game you bet on: Is there more value in the point spread or the money line? The answer to that question is based on your assessment of two things:

1. Is this team likely to win but not cover?
2. Is this team likely to cover but not win?

From there it's a matter of doing some simple analysis and finding out where the value lies.

A Little Money Line Math

Let's start with a question. Which of these bets would you prefer to place?

a) $300 to win $100 on a heavy favorite (-300) with a 75 percent chance of winning

b) $150 to win $100 on a medium favorite (-150) with a 60 percent chance of winning

c) $100 to win $200 on an underdog (+200) with a 33.33 percent chance of winning

This is a trick question to show that value can be found on either side of the money line, depending on the odds posted and a team's chances of winning. The correct answer is that each scenario is essentially the same, with an expected return of zero, so you should have no preference among each of these bets. (Note: The chance of winning is based on the bettor's own analysis, experience, knowledge and judgment — just like determining at what price to buy or sell a stock.)

To understand how it works, just apply the following formula:

(Chance of Winning x Amount to Be Won) - (Amount Bet x the Chance of Losing).

The result is your expected return.

In (a), 75 percent of the time you win $100, but you lose $300 the other 25% percent.

Expected return = (.75 x 100) - (.25 x 300) = 75 - 75 = 0

In (b), 60 percent of the time you win $100, but you lose $150 the other 40 percent.

Expected return = (.60 x 100) - (.40 x 150) = 60 - 60 = 0

In (c), 33.33 percent of the time you win $200, but you lose $100 the other 66.66 percent.

Expected return = (.3333 x 200) - (.6666 x 100) = 66.66 - 66.66 = 0

You can see the pattern. To calculate the percentage of wins required to break even for any money line, use the following formula, which was introduced in the previous section on proposition bets:

Required Win Percent = Amount Risked ÷ (Amount Risked + Amount of Win)

So for example, a line of -110 implies a risk of $110 to win $100. Applying our equation we get:

Required Win Percent = 110 ÷ (110 + 100) = 110 ÷ 210 = 52.38%

To save you from doing this math, I have included Table 9.1, which reports the Required Win Percent for a number of money lines.

Table 9.1

MONEY LINE PROBABILITY CHART

Money Line	Loss	Win	Win % Required
-320	-320	100	76.19%
-300	-300	100	75.00%
-280	-280	100	73.68%
-270	-270	100	72.97%
-260	-260	100	72.22%
-250	-250	100	71.43%
-240	-240	100	70.59%

-230	-230	100	69.70%
-220	-220	100	68.75%
-210	-210	100	67.74%
-200	-200	100	66.67%
-180	-180	100	64.29%
-170	-170	100	62.96%
-160	-160	100	61.54%
-150	-150	100	60.00%
-140	-140	100	58.33%
-130	-130	100	56.52%
-120	-120	100	54.55%
-110	-110	100	52.38%
-105	-105	100	51.22%
-100	-100	100	50.00%
105	-100	105	48.78%
110	-100	110	47.62%
120	-100	120	45.45%
130	-100	130	43.48%
140	-100	140	41.67%
150	-100	150	40.00%
160	-100	160	38.46%
170	-100	170	37.04%
180	-100	180	35.71%
200	-100	200	33.33%
210	-100	210	32.26%
220	-100	220	31.25%
230	-100	230	30.30%
240	-100	240	29.41%
250	-100	250	28.57%
260	-100	260	27.78%

270	-100	270	27.03%
280	-100	280	26.32%
290	-100	290	25.64%
300	-100	300	25.00%

Just a quick note to make sure you are clear on the chart: Have a look at the line for -180. If you lose, you lose $180, but a win gets you only $100. Thus you need to win 64.29 percent of the time to break even. Similarly, looking at +170, you see a loss costs you only $100, but a win gains $170, so you need to win only 37.04 percent of the time. This is an important chart because it works for all football, basketball and baseball money lines.

Why is this important? Simple. Every time you look at a money line, you need to know the Required Winning Percent to break even. If you expect the -300 favorite from (a) to win 80 percent of the time, than you've got a betting opportunity. If you expect (a) to win only 70 percent of the time, you should move on to the next game or think about betting on the team on the other side of the money line. Returning to the NFL example where Denver is -160 and Miami +140, you see (using the money line probability chart) that the Required Win Percent for Denver is 61.54% and for Miami it is 41.67%.

So which is a better bet: Denver or Miami? There is no right answer. Some bettors prefer to play underdogs and small favorites using the money line, while others like the big favorites. Both can be right and both can be wrong; it simply depends on your analysis of the game. Although some bettors often shy away from big favorites, you don't have to. Rob Gillespie, former operations manager of the Bodog sports books, remarks, "I have seen occasions where a baseball team closed as a -210 favorite or higher on 12 occasions in one month and they won 10 of those games. Betting to win $100 on those 12 games would have meant risking a total of $2,915, but you would have made a decent return of $435."

Now let's compare a spread to a money line. Although each sports book is different, Table 9.2 presents the chart that most sports books use as a guideline for converting point spreads to money lines for the NFL. College football is slightly different, and that conversion chart is presented in the College Football Playbook.

Table 9.2

NFL POINT SPREAD TO MONEY LINE CONVERSION CHART

Favorite Point Spread	Corresponding Money Line
-2	-130/+110
-2.5	-140/+120
-3	-155/+135
-3.5	-175/+155
-4	-200/+170
-4.5	-220/+180
-5/-5.5	-240/+190
-6	-270/+210
-6.5	-300/+220
-7	-330/+250
-7.5/-8/-8.5	-360/+280
-9/-9.5	-400/+300
-10	-450/+325
-11	-550/+375
-12	-600/+400
-13	-650/+450

Table 9.2 allows you to compare the point spread to the money line to see if there is an inconsistency that could provide sports betting value. Moreover, you can use it to convert your own point spreads for NFL games,

calculated using the Value Rating and Score Sheet methods presented in Chapter Five, into money lines.

NFL money lines aren't traditionally offered for point spreads outside the 2-14 range because at those extremes it becomes difficult for sports books to balance the betting action. If a spread moves from -1.5 to -1, they don't have much room to move on the money line. Players will simply ignore betting the +1 and take the underdog at +105 or even, lowering the commission for the sports book. Above 14, the money lines are just too high. Bettors seldom take the big price, and the sports book exposes itself to a significant loss when big upsets happen.

Money Line Value

Because the general betting public is uninformed (especially about money lines), sports books earn extra profits on money lines, especially when a point spread favorite wins but doesn't cover. Imagine an NFL game involving Kansas City and San Diego. Let's say the original point spread moved from Chargers -3.5 when it was posted early in the week to Chargers -4 by kickoff. However, the money line didn't move from -175/+155, where it was originally posted when the Chargers were -3.5.

According to Table 9.2, the NFL Point Spread to Money Line Conversion Chart, the money line should have been -200/+170 at game time (reflecting the -4 point spread). But the betting public didn't seem to care, and bet heavily on the underdog Chiefs at +155 in hopes of winning big and collecting $155 on a $100 bet. When the favored Chargers edged the Chiefs 35-34 on a last-minute touchdown drive, the sports books were in a win-win situation. They collected their normal commission on the point spread and paid out nothing on the money line proposition. An Intelligent Bettor (using the conversion chart) would have spotted the mispricing and recognized the added value of taking a contrarian position. He would have placed a money line bet on the Chargers at -175, picking up an additional .5 points in value, which ended up being the difference between a winning and losing bet.

So when assessing your bets, compare the money line and the point spread to find discrepancies like this that you can exploit to your advantage.

Not every money line will present an opportunity, but be sure to compare the money line to the corresponding spread using the conversion chart. With the money line, it's not how often you are correct that matters (as it is with the point spread); it's the *magnitude* of correctness, because of the leverage involved in picking the winner. Or as the great Al Davis said, "Just win, baby."

Remember, it doesn't matter how big the price or how much you get back, as long as you keep your bet sizes equal to 5 percent of your betting capital and know the Required Win Percent so you can determine on which side of the money line to place your bet.

Baseball Uses the Money Line

Betting on baseball is different than wagering on football or basketball. Because many baseball games are decided by a run or two, it's not practical to have a point spread. So instead of the point spread, the money line is the primary wagering line quoted for baseball.

Here is an example of a typical baseball money line:

```
Red Sox -120
John Lester
Yankees +110
C.C. Sabathia
```

The money line determines the amount of money that must be bet when wagering on either the favorite or the underdog, based on a $100 win. The highest negative money line determines the favorite team; the lowest negative money line — and all positive money lines — determines the underdog. The most common case is the favorite with a negative line and the underdog with a positive line. While the money line for baseball may look confusing to the novice player, it is easy to figure out.

In this example, if you wanted to bet on the Red Sox, who are the favorites, you would be putting up $120. If you win you collect $220, giving you a $100 profit. In other words, you risk $120 to make $100.

If you wanted to take the underdog Yankees, you would wager $100 and collect $210 if you won. This means you risk $100 to make $110.

Recall earlier in this chapter that every time you look at a money line, you need to ask, "What Required Win Percent is necessary to break even?" Referencing the Money Line Probability Chart (Table 9.1), the Required Win Percent for the Red Sox -120 is 54.55%. For the Yankees +110, the Required Win Percent is 47.62%. So if your analysis shows the Yankees winning this game 60 percent of the time, take the +110 with confidence.

The Basics of Baseball Betting: Is It Hitting or Pitching?

There are two schools of thought when it comes to analyzing a baseball line. One says pitching is so important in determining the line that to win bets you must primarily analyze the pitching. The pitcher is involved in every play, while even a key slugger like Adrian Gonzalez might be involved in just four at-bats and a couple of plays in the field. Moreover, big hitters often get days off with no notice. But John Lester pitches to as many as 40 guys in a single game. That's why many bettors analyze the starters' statistics for recent games and then consider bullpens before even looking at offensive numbers. Bettors who rely on listed pitchers are rarely surprised in a bad way.

The contrarian school of thought states that because pitching is already so analyzed by sports books in determining the line, there is not much you can do to find value. Instead, these contrarians focus on finding value in the analysis of offensive production.

Both strategies make sense. Both require discipline and good analytical skills. The right answer ultimately rests in where you can find the biggest edge and the most value. It's only after working through some actual examples with a pencil and a sheet of paper that you will able to see what works best for you. Sparky Anderson once said, "Good pitching beats good hitting." But it's up to you to figure out what "good pitching" and "good hitting" are.

The specifics of Major League Baseball betting are covered in detail in the Major League Baseball Playbook.

Pay Attention to Starting Pitching

In baseball, sports books set the money line based on the starting pitcher. That's why the names of the pitchers are included in the line. In the event of a pitching change just before a game, the money line may be adjusted. You can bet a baseball game several ways, depending on the pitching. In the Yankees–Red Sox game above, the money line was based on John Lester going for the Red Sox and C.C. Sabathia for the Yankees. You can bet on this in four ways:

1. An *action* bet, which means the bet is live no matter if the pitchers are changed before the game or not. If there is an unscheduled pitching change, the payout may be different than the odds posted for the starting money line, but the bet is still active. So for an action bet, it doesn't matter who the starting pitchers are.

2. A *both* bet is canceled if one or both of the starting pitchers listed when you make your bet doesn't make the start. In that case, the bet is voided and the wager returned. So for Red Sox–Yankees, both Lester and Sabathia must start.

3. An *on* bet is where the pitcher of just the visiting team must start. Since the Red Sox are visiting, if you wanted to bet on the Red Sox with Lester pitching and don't care who the Yankees pitcher is, your bet would be active as long as Lester starts. If Lester does not start, the bet is voided and the wager returned.

4. An *against* bet is where the pitcher of just the home team must start. Since the Yankees are home, if you want to bet on the Yankees with Sabathia pitching and don't care who the Red Sox pitcher is, then your bet would be active as long as Sabathia starts. If Sabathia does not start, the bet is voided and the wager returned.

Which option should you choose? Well, there is no simple answer. It really depends on your reason for picking the Red Sox or the Yankees. If you take the Red Sox because you noticed they are a good road team, then the starting pitchers don't really weigh heavily in your analysis, so *action* is the choice for you. Likewise if you emphasize offensive numbers in your analysis.

But if you like the Red Sox because you favor a groundball pitcher (or left-hander) against the Yankees, regardless of who the New York pitcher is, then you would want to take the *on* bet and make sure your bet only has action if Lester starts.

If you choose to bet on the Yankees because you think Sabathia beats the Red Sox no matter who pitches for Boston, then the *against* bet is the choice to make.

Most bettors prefer to take starting pitching into consideration, at least in part, so a *both* bet is the most common choice. While starting-pitching changes are not that common, especially in the last few minutes before a start, it usually makes sense to take advantage of the both option to prevent a frustrating loss if a pitcher tweaks a hamstring or gets a blister while warming up. Also, if you are betting on overnight lines or before you go to work in the morning, there is a greater chance of a listed-pitching change than there is if you are able to wait until just before game time to place your bet. You should also note that doubleheaders are slightly more prone to late starting-pitching changes than other games, as managers occasionally elect to change the order of the two pitchers for the day at the last minute.

Using listed pitchers may affect only a handful of wagers each year, but if using them to your advantage prevents any of those plays from being a losing bet, why take the chance?

Baseball's Dime Line — A Bettor's Bargain

Keep in mind that sports books make money on bets by collecting a commission, the vig, on every bet made. The vig is the difference between what is wagered and what is won. In baseball betting, the sports books make their money when the favorite team loses. In our example, if the Red Sox lose, the sports book makes $10. They are collecting $120 for the losing bet but paying out only $110 for the winning bet. The sports book will adjust the line if one team is heavily favored, to make it more enticing to bet the underdog and balance their own books.

Our example is what is known as a dime line. That simply refers to the difference between the underdog price and the favorite price. In this case the Red Sox are -120 and the Yankees are +110, which is called 10 cents, or a dime.

Some sports books use a 20-cent, or "wide," line. Still others use a graduated line, which starts out as a 10-cent line but increases as the price increases. If a favorite is -115, a sports book with a graduated line would have +105 on the underdog. However, if they have a favorite as -180, they would likely have the underdog at +160, whereas the dime line book would have +170.

Whether you bet on the underdog or the favorite, you always get a better deal with a 10-cent line than a 20-cent line because you are paying less commission. An even better deal is a five-cent, or "nickel," line, if you can find one. Over the course of a baseball season, saving that kind of money every time you bet will mean more money in your pocket and less in the sports book's. Simply: You win *more* when you win, and you lose *less* when you lose. Fortunately for baseball bettors, many sports books offer dime lines and occasionally nickel lines, so it pays to shop around.

Why Is Baseball So Good for Sports Bettors?

Baseball presents a great opportunity for bettors in part because the vig charged by the sports books is generally lower than for other sports. The dime line in baseball has to be the best deal in all of sports wagering — except for the nickel line. The reason for the discounting is that summer is traditionally a quiet time in the betting world, so sports books hungry for business make baseball as attractive as possible.

Second, not only do you get the best value when betting, you also get to impose conditions on your wagers. When you bet on football, your bet goes even if the starting quarterback for your team sprains his ankle in warm-ups; likewise when betting basketball, you can't get your money back if the starting point guard gets food poisoning an hour before tip-off. Consider an NFL game where Aaron Rodgers is questionable because he has a knee injury. Wouldn't it be great if you could place a bet conditional on his starting? Or a bet on the Packers' opponent that would be conditional on Rodgers' not entering the game? Of course it would, but that is not an option for football... yet.

Third, the baseball regular season has nearly 10 times as many games as the NFL (2,430 to 256) and roughly twice as many as the NBA. All those extra games are extra betting opportunities.

Betting on Props, Totals and Money Lines Means More Opportunities

There are profitable and sensible betting opportunities that exist beyond point spreads, so the challenge is not to limit your chances to profit. During the NFL season, you've got 16 games to bet on each week. By including money lines and totals with the point spreads on each game, you have expanded your weekly betting opportunities to 48. Consider the "Poisson Props" and you will discover even more chances for potential profit. Add in baseball's 2,430 regular season games and your betting opportunities really take off. If you're only betting NFL football point spreads and the occasional basketball game, your opportunities are limited. By considering the many hidden treasures discussed in this chapter, you will increase your odds of achieving sports wagering success as well as your enjoyment of the games.

Buyer Beware — The Seven Deadly Bets

As I am constantly telling my financial clients, when an offer seems too good to be true, it usually is. This advice also applies to sports wagering. When you start to see larger and larger offers of a payout for a winning pick, always assume the odds are against you. In sports betting, these bets are often called exotics. They are cloaked in complexity and are generally the wagers you want to avoid. Exotics include parlays, teasers, sweethearts and futures. While football cards (explained below) are fun to play with your friends, the Intelligent Bettor steers clear of them too. In baseball, run lines can add some additional intrigue, but the extra commission charge isn't worth it. Finally, if you are serious about sports wagering, don't limit your betting opportunities to the nationally televised games.

Parlays

Let's start by taking a look at one of the most common — and alluring — exotic bets: the parlay. A parlay is simply a combination bet, and in fact it's often called a *combo*. In these wagers, a group of otherwise independent bets are linked, and all must win for the parlay to pay. The most common parlay involves linking point spread bets in two or more games (up to a maximum of 12) in a single wager. But a parlay can also link totals bets, proposition bets and other wagers. Thus a parlay could involve only two teams playing one game, with the bettor wagering on the point spreads for each team as well as the total. But whether the parlay involves two teams, two games, four games or more, all the selections must win for the parlay to win. Sports books express their parlay odds in terms of "teams," regardless of whether the wagers being linked are point spreads, proposition bets and/or totals. Thus a "four-team" parlay quote represents the odds associated with four linked bets of any type.

Clearly it is more difficult to pick the correct outcome for more events, so the payoff, and the odds against winning it, increase with the number of events chosen. Instead of making five or more separate bets on a series of five different games, a bettor places a single parlay bet, hoping he can correctly predict the outcome of all five games. Parlays are by far the most popular exotic wager because they appear to offer the potential for a big payoff for a small wager. If you place a four-team parlay, going 3-1 isn't any better than going 0-4. All of your bets must win, or at least tie, for you to win.

Most parlays are what are called fixed-odds parlay payouts. These involve football and basketball point spreads and totals at standard odds. Instead of calculating the odds of each particular parlay, most sports books use a standard set of fixed-odds payoffs for such parlays.

Table 10.1 shows the typical sports book payouts for football and basketball parlays:

Table 10.1

Parlay Odds

2 Team Parlay	2.6 to 1 (often stated as: 13 to 5)
3 Team Parlay	6 to 1
4 Team Parlay	10 to 1
5 Team Parlay	20 to 1
6 Team Parlay	40 to 1
7 Team Parlay	75 to 1

8 Team Parlay	100 to 1
9 Team Parlay	150 to 1
10 Team Parlay	300 to 1

How do you read Table 10.1? Simple. Suppose you bet on a six-team parlay. If you win the bet (by picking all six winners correctly) you get 40 to 1 on your money. So a $10 bet on a six-team parlay bet would pay out $400 in winnings.

There are some conditions associated with parlay bets that every bettor should know. Although the conditions applied to parlays vary by sports book, the following are a few general rules:

1. If you lose any game on your parlay bet, the entire bet loses.
2. If you bet a two-game parlay and any of the games ties the spread, the parlay becomes a straight bet (essentially the game that ties is null and you get standard odds on your remaining game).
3. If one game results in a push in a multi-contest parlay, you don't lose: The parlay drops down to the next payout level. For example, a four-game parlay with a one-game push becomes a three-game parlay. Likewise, a 10-game parlay with a one-game push becomes a nine-game parlay. If two games tie the spread, you subtract two games from your parlay game total: A six-game parlay bet with two pushes becomes a four-game parlay.
4. Most sports books specify a maximum payout on any one parlay bet, usually $100,000. This provision is meant to protect the sports book from paying out a huge win. The maximum payout rule is a sports book's insurance policy against runaway parlay bet wins.

Now let's do the math and compare a parlay to a straight point spread bet at the standard 11-to-10 odds. A parlay can be viewed as a series of straight point spread bets where the winnings from one bet are automatically rolled over and bet again on another game.[50] Even though I would

---

50 This is a fundamental flaw of a parlay bet. A parlay is structured to systematically increase your bet size until you either win it all or bust completely. Recall from Chapter Six that it is essential to keep your bet sizes the same to avoid the wipeout. Consistently

never recommend rolling over your profits from one winning bet to the next because it constantly increases your bet size (violating a basic principle of the *Get In and Win* System), I will present the math so you can understand why a parlay is such a bad deal.

Consider a two-game parlay where $110 is wagered on Team A to win the first game. Upon winning Game One, the winnings and the original capital totaling $210 ($110 original capital plus $100 winnings) are immediately bet on Team B in Game Two, resulting in an additional $190.91 of winnings. After two games, the total amount accumulated is $400.91 ($100 Game One winnings + $190.91 Game Two winnings + $110 original bet amount). Now compare the $400.91 total amount accumulated from the two straight bets to the amount returned on a two-game parlay bet. Using the preceding chart, a two-game parlay pays 2.6 to 1 for a total return of $396 (2.6 x $110 = $286 winnings + 110 original bet). Therefore, combining two straight point spread bets is a better deal than playing a two-team parlay.

Table 10.2 compares the amount accumulated (the original bet plus the winnings) from a series of winning point spread bets at standard 11-to-10 odds to the returns available from the corresponding parlay bet:

Table 10.2

Rolling Over Straight Bets versus Parlays

Bet Amount $110.00

Straight Bet		**Parlay**		
# Games	Total Returned	# Games	Payout Odds	Total Returned
1	210	1		N/A
2	401	2	2.6 to 1	396
3	765	3	6 to 1	770

playing the parlays dooms you to suffering the same fate as Streaking Steve, who was introduced in Chapter Two.

4	1,461	4	10 to 1	1,210
5	2,789	5	20 to 1	2,310
6	5,325	6	40 to 1	4,510
7	10,167	7	75 to 1	8,360
8	19,409	8	100 to 1	11,110
9	37,054	9	150 to 1	16,610
10	70,739	10	300 to 1	33,110

It's clear from Table 10.2 that for parlays involving more than three games, the returns for the sports bettor get increasingly worse when compared to making straight bets and rolling over the profits.

While it would seem that parlays of more than three teams should do very well for sports books, keep in mind that the books don't always take in enough to cover the payout. And the book sometimes has to cover much, if not all, of a winning bet from its own reserves. While it is relatively easy for a sports book to balance the betting action on one game, it is very difficult to evenly split the action in parlays involving multiple games. In addition to that, sports books often see the same picks over and over in different parlays. So in order to cover the risk of having to pay out the infrequent very large bet, the books charge a higher commission fee. Remember the odds shown are just the Vegas standard; there is an almost infinite range of different payout schemes above the standard 2.6/1 and 6/1 for two- to three-team parlays.

With parlays you can also combine point spreads, totals and even different types of bets. To understand how a parlay works when combining different types of bets, let's look at a simple two-team parlay with an example from an imaginary football game, in this case Tampa Bay at San Francisco. Let's say the line for the game is San Francisco -3.5 and the total was 36. Parlaying the point spread and the total gives four possible combinations:

1. San Francisco -3.5 and Over 36
2. San Francisco -3.5 and Under 36
3. Tampa Bay +3.5 and Over 36
4. Tampa Bay +3.5 and Under 36

Ignoring ties, only one of these will be the winner.

Now, let's assume four players each bet $100 on a different one of the four possible outcomes for the parlay, and Parlay Four is the winner. The house would collect $100 from the three people who didn't pick the right result and would pay $260 to the one person who had. That guy would also get his risk money back. The sports book would collect $400 in total, and pay out $360 for a net profit of $40, which is a 10 percent commission rate for its services.

With three-team parlays the calculation remains the same, except now there are eight possible outcomes and the payoff is 6-1. With $100 bets on each outcome, books would collect $700 from the losing plays and pay out $600 to the winner, for a net profit of $100 on $800 collected — a 12.5 percent commission. Table 10.3 reports standard fixed-odds parlay payouts showing the number of teams involved, the payout and the sports book's commission percentage.

Table 10.3

# of Teams	Payout	Sports Book Commission
2	2.6 to 1	10.0%
3	6 to 1	12.5%
4	10 to 1	31.3%
5	20 to 1	34.4%
6	40 to 1	35.9%
7	75 to 1	40.6%
8	100 to 1	40.8%
9	150 to 1	41.0%
10	300 to 1	41.2%

Since sports books earn a much higher commission on parlay bets than on straight point spread bets,[51] sports books are happy to offer parlays of all kinds, and count on the illusion of a larger payoff to distract uninformed sports bettors from the considerably worse chance of winning. The distraction works — otherwise the sports books wouldn't still be offering them. Avoid the parlays and the higher commissions if you want to keep more of your betting capital in your pocket.

Teasers

Teasers are another type of parlay and are one of the ways the sports books try to convince you that you can shave the odds a little more in your favor. The name of this bet should be enough to keep sensible bettors away. In the dictionary, the word *tease* is defined as "to disturb or annoy with persistent petty requests."

However, every year the number of bettors that wager on teaser bets grows.

A teaser is a wager where the bettor may move the point spread a given number of points in his favor on two or more games, provided the games are played together in a parlay. A teaser is basically a parlay where sports bettors have some control of the line on each pick *in exchange for a lower payout*. There are many variations, but generally you can alter (or tease) your football lines 6, 6.5 or 7 points, and your basketball lines 4, 4.5 or 5 points. The number of bets in the parlay and the number of points selected determines the payout odds. The greater the number of points teased, the worse the odds become.

To get a better idea of how a teaser works, let's look at an imaginary two-game teaser in the NFL with the Patriots -8 in a game versus the Colts and the Chiefs +2 versus the Raiders. For these games, let's say you like these numbers — sort of. You aren't really sure the Patriots will win by more than a touchdown playing against Peyton Manning's high-powered offense or that the Chiefs can keep it close against the Raiders, their archrival. So

---

51 The commission rate for a point spread bet is approximately 9.1%.

you can tease both these picks. If you teased 7 points you would have a two-game teaser with Patriots -1 and the Chiefs +9. I think you can clearly see that making New England have to win by only 2 (instead of 9) to cover makes this bet easier to win. Also, the Broncos can now lose by up to 8 and still cover. The trade-off is a reduced payout. While the exact amount of the change in the payout varies from book to book, it wouldn't be unreasonable for the teaser to pay 10/13 compared to 13/5 for a standard parlay. If you risked $65, a winning teaser pays $50 — but the same two picks in a winning parlay would pay $169.

Another negative of teaser bets is that a push (or a tie) in one of the games counts as a loss at many sports books, thus in the event of a push the sports book pockets all the money and pays out nothing. At other books, with teasers involving three or more picks, a push on any one part of it reduces the payout to the next-lowest level: A four-teamer where one game is a push would pay out at three-team levels, etc. Note that a two-team teaser with a push is not reduced to a one-team teaser because there is no such thing. Ties are handled differently by each sports book, so make sure you know the rules if you decide to wager on a teaser. The bottom line is, beware of the teasers, or you can find yourself in real trouble.

Sweethearts

The sweetheart is another type of teaser. These bets give you even more points in your teaser (say 10 or 13 for football), but you must pick more games, the payouts are further reduced, and all pushes make your bet a loser. What gets bettors to go for teasers and sweethearts are the close games they remember losing by just a point or two. The lure of getting extra points on games becomes too much for many bettors to pass up. Teasers and sweethearts are a key source of income for many sports books. In fact, sports books make far more money per dollar bet on teasers and sweethearts than they do on straight bets because of the much lower payout. For teaser and sweetheart bets, the extra points you get are more than offset by the reduced odds you must give.

Football Cards

Football cards are the lottery tickets of sports betting — that is, bettors try to make a lot of money on a minimal investment. Football parlay cards are extremely popular among local bookies, operating illegally. They might look like this:

For Amusement Only   For Amusement Only

Lucky Lenney's
Fantasy Parlay Card 5/26/98 thru 06/01/98

| FAVORITE | (home team in bold) | UNDERDOG |

Pro Football Sunday December 21 1997

	FAVORITE			UNDERDOG	
1	Dallas	- 2.5	2	NY Giants	+ 2.5
3	UNDER	37.5	4	OVER	37.5
5	Tennessee	- 2.5	6	Pittsburgh	+ 2.5
7	UNDER	40.5	8	OVER	40.5
9	Washington	- 5.5	10	Philadelphia	+ 5.5
11	UNDER	37.5	12	OVER	37.5
13	Kansas City	- 7.5	14	New Orleans	+ 7.5
15	UNDER	36.5	16	OVER	36.5
17	Minnesota	- 6.5	18	Indianapolis	+ 6.5
19	UNDER	42.5	20	OVER	42.5
21	Cincinnati	- 7	22	Baltimore	+ 7
23	UNDER	48	24	OVER	48
25	Tampa Bay	- 7.5	26	Chicago	+ 7.5
27	UNDER	35.5	28	OVER	35.5
29	Jacksonville	- 4.5	30	Oakland	+ 4.5
31	UNDER	46.5	32	OVER	46.5
33	Denver	- 13.5	34	San Deigo	+ 13.5
35	UNDER	41.5	36	OVER	41.5
37	Detroit	- 6.5	38	NY Giants	+ 6.5
39	UNDER	43.5	40	OVER	43.5
41	Atlanta	- 3.5	42	Arizona	+ 3.5
43	UNDER	42.5	44	OVER	42.5
45	San Francisco	- 2.5	46	Seattle	+ 2.5
47	UNDER	42.5	48	OVER	42.5

All Fantasy cards must be submitted no later than Friday midnite. Any tie will decrease number of games played by one. Minimum 3 picks, max 10 no more than 2000 points will be paid on this card. All games must be played on the above scheduled date or they are not counted as plays.

3 of 3 pays 5 for 1	4 of 4 pays 10 for 1
6 of 6 pays 25 for 1	7 of 7 pays 40 for 1
9 of 9 pays 75 for 1	10 of 10 pays 100 for 1

5 of 5 pays 15 for 1
8 of 8 pays 50 for 1
9 of 10 pays 25 for 1

Loser special
5 of 6 pays 2 for 1   0 of 6 pays 2 for 1   0 of 10 pays 10 for 1

(CIRCLE your choices - Please keep the top section - turn in the bottom to register for contest)

1	2	3	4	5	6	7	8	9	10	11	12
13	14	15	16	17	18	19	20	21	22	23	24	25
26	27	28	29	30	31	32	33	34	35	36	37	38
39	40	41	42	43	44	45	46	47	48	49	50	51
52	53	54	55	56	57	58	59	60	61	62	63	64
65	66	87	68	69	70	71	72	73	74	75	76	77
78	79	80	81	82	83	84	85	86	87	88	89	90

Name _____   Hm PH _____

Number of games _____   Amount of points bet _____

Football cards are a version of parlay bets offered by sports books. The basic difference between parlay bets and football cards is usually in the payouts, with the sports book typically offering better odds than the local bookie, although both provide a much lower payout than can be earned by merely rolling over the winnings from a series of straight odds bets (which isn't a good idea either). Specifically, a five-game parlay offered at a sports book will typically pay 20 to 1, while the local bookie's football card may only offer 15 to 1.

Table 10.4 below compares the typical payouts on football cards to sports books parlays, and the results of rolling over the profits from a series of winning straight bets. As you can see, the payouts for football cards are consistently worse.

Table 10.4

# of Games	Football Card	Sports Book Parlay	Series of Straight Bets
3	5 to 1	6 to 1	6 to 1
4	10 to 1	10 to 1	12 to 1
5	15 to 1	20 to 1	24 to 1
6	25 to 1	40 to 1	47 to 1
7	40 to 1	75 to 1	91 to 1
8	50 to 1	100 to 1	175 to 1
9	75 to 1	150 to 1	336 to 1
10	100 to 1	300 to 1	642 to 1

The way in which ties are handled is another difference between football cards and parlay bets. Sports books offering parlay bets will often reduce the number of games selected in the parlay when one game in the parlay ties against the point spread. For example, if you have a six-game parlay at a sports book and one game ties, you will then have a five-game parlay and will receive a reduced payout based on a five-game parlay should your other games win.

Local bookies aren't usually as generous on ties. They typically count them as a loss, which then makes the entire football card worthless. To make matters worse, local bookies typically adjust the odds a bit, hoping for ties. For this reason, you will see the majority of point spreads on football cards falling on the key numbers, like 3, 4, 6, 7, 10, 13, 14, 17 and 21 (The NFL's key numbers are discussed in Chapter Seven). If the Las Vegas line has a team favored by 9 points, the local bookie might use 10 on the football card because more games are decided by 10 points than by 9 points.

Another trick some bookies use on football cards is to offer payouts such as 10 *for* 1 as opposed to 10 *to* 1. A $10 parlay winner at 10-for-1 odds would return $100, while at 10-to-1 the return would be $110 ($10 original bet plus $100 winnings). So it pays to read the fine print on football cards.

Parlay cards can be a fun, inexpensive way to enjoy a little action on the weekend's games, but they are a poor wagering proposition.

Baseball's Run Lines

Baseball run lines are essentially a combination of the point spread and the money line rolled into one. The run line normally uses a constant spread of 1.5 runs. The team that is favored on the money line will also be the favored team on the run line.

Why is the spread always -1.5 runs? It's because baseball games cannot end in a tie, so a spread of -.5 would have no impact and a spread of -1 would result in a push a large portion of the time (approximately 27 percent of MLB games are decided by one run). By making the run line -1.5 runs, the favorite team is forced to win by at least 2 runs and some real intrigue is added to the wager. When wagering run lines, both listed pitchers must start and the game must go 8.5 innings.

Understanding baseball run lines is easier with an example. On the regular money line you may see odds like:

Boston Red Sox	**+160**
New York Yankees	**-170**

This indicates that Yankee bettors are risking $170 to win $100, while Red Sox bettors will risk $100 to win $160.

But for the same game, the run line might look something like:

Boston Red Sox	**+1.5**	**-140**
New York Yankees	**-1.5**	**+120**

Now with the run line, the Red Sox bettors are risking more money than they will win, in this case $140 to win $100, but in return they are receiving 1.5 runs. Even if the Red Sox lose by one run, those betting Boston on the run line will win their bet because of the additional 1.5 runs, whereas Yankee bettors are now risking $100 to win $120.

So in exchange for the extra risk of accepting a 1.5-run handicap on the favorite team, bettors are rewarded with a much better payout. On the other hand, betting the underdog using the run line has the opposite effect — you win more often (the one-run losses become wins after you consider the additional 1.5 runs received). But when the underdog wins outright, the run line payout is less than the money line return. There is no exact formula for converting money lines to run lines, as it depends on the pitchers and teams involved. And the only time there is a difference in the betting outcome between a run line and money line wager is when the favorite team wins by exactly one run.

In football and basketball point spreads, the odds are usually at a standard of -110 and the point spread itself is typically moved to balance action. For baseball, the spread is fixed at -1.5 runs and the attached odds are changed to balance action. As an example, consider a basketball game where the Mavericks are -1.5 favorites and there is a lot of betting action on them; the line will move to -2 and then -2.5 in an effort to get bettors to wager on the other team. However, in baseball, if the Dodgers were a

-1.5 (-110) favorite and the betting action was coming in heavy on them, the run line would be moved to -1.5 (-115) and then -1.5 (-120) to balance the action.

The problem with the run line is that the sports book's commission is higher than it is for the money line. Recall from Chapter Nine that one of the benefits of betting baseball is the reduced commission, or the dime line. The sports books' take on the run line is approximately double the amount typically charged on the money line. While the run line is not a terrible bet like a teaser or a sweetheart, stay with the money line instead of the run line and you will keep your sports betting commissions low, resulting in a higher return for you.

The Futures Are Not Good

In the financial markets, people make money (and lose it) all the time by trading on futures. They do this by contracting to buy specific quantities of a commodity or financial instrument at a particular price, with delivery set at a specified time in the future. They then usually resell it if the price changes in their favor. If you have enough information and experience with whatever you are buying, it is possible to make reasonable, informed judgments and decrease your trading risk.

That's not quite how it works in sports betting. Here futures are odds posted in advance on who will win various major sporting events, like the Super Bowl, World Series, NBA Championship and NCAA Basketball Tournament. You can also find futures quotes for division and conference champions in professional and college sports. There are also more exotic futures — betting whether a team will go over or under a certain amount of wins for the season, whether a quarterback will throw for the most yards during the season, whether a running back will get the most yards rushed in a season, and so on. These odds are not based on actual information but almost entirely on the wagering activity at the sports book in question. As a result, the lines vary considerably. But the line can be reliable: In April 2011 the Cubs were 50:1 to win the World Series. On the other hand, Pittsburgh was 500:1 — not an unrealistic assessment to be sure, but a more fact-based line would likely put the odds closer to those of winning a megamillion-dollar lottery.

With futures, the odds are tilted heavily in favor of the sports book. How do we know this? Well, one simple way to tell if a bet is fair is whether or not you can take the other side of the bet. In this case, you cannot bet against a futures quote. You can bet on a team to win the World Series, but you can't bet *against* a team to win it. What does it tell you when the book won't let you pick from both sides of a proposition?

If this weren't enough to steer you clear of futures, you should also remember what such a bet will *prevent* you from doing. Futures bets usually aren't decided for months, so putting money on one ties up your sports betting capital for a significant period of time. This is costing you the opportunity to use that money on other bets that are almost certainly more in your favor.

TV: There's a Reason They Call It the Idiot Box

Bettors also get lured into making foolish bets because they are actually going to see the game — whether in person or on TV (but mostly on TV). Now, it is not surprising that we like to wager on games we are going to watch: It's a lot of fun and more emotionally engaging to watch a game that you have a direct stake in. That said, here is something to consider that may save you money in the long run.

Sports books give equal time and weight to setting the point spread on each and every college and pro football game played on any weekend. The Intelligent Bettor does something very similar. However, as we know, not all bettors are intelligent. In fact, a fair number of them start their handicapping with the TV guide and bet only on televised games. By some estimates, nationally televised games account for as much as 50 percent of the betting each weekend. By ignoring low-profile matches that aren't on network TV or ESPN, couch potatoes miss out on moneymaking opportunities.

Remember that even though all the advertising would like to tell you differently, Monday Night Football and the Super Bowl are just games. The

Intelligent Bettor recognizes that (despite their popularity) these games offer the same opportunity for sports betting profit as a mid-major conference football game between East Carolina and Marshall. That is the attitude you need to succeed as a bettor. Do not limit your bets to televised games, and don't bet every televised game if you want to show a long-term profit.

Don't Be a Pig

There's an old Wall Street adage that goes something like this: "Bulls make money. Bears make money. Pigs get slaughtered." By ignoring the exotic bets and wagering only when you find betting value with an appropriate Margin of Safety, you will keep the odds of success on your side and avoid the disastrous wipeout.

In summary, to consistently place winning wagers: Keep it simple; get the right information; search for value; practice careful money management; stay disciplined; and bet only when there is an adequate Margin of Safety. Remember, *"Money won is twice as sweet as money earned."* Good luck, prepare properly and have fun!

Glossary of *Get In and Win* Sports Wagering Terms

Beginning Capital

The initial amount of money that a sports bettor sets aside at the beginning of each year or season for sports wagering.

Five Percent Rule

There is one and only one appropriate bet size for each wager. That amount is 5 percent of your Beginning Capital and is an absolute fixed dollar amount that is calculated at the beginning of each season and stays fixed at that level for the entire season.

Money Management Game Plan

See the Five Percent Rule.

Margin of Safety

The difference between your calculated point spread and the sports book's point spread. It represents a cushion that provides protection against the unexpected — either unanticipated team performance or the unlikely game-changing play: a blocked field goal that is returned for a touchdown, a basketball team shooting 70 percent from behind the 3-point line, or a baseball team scoring the walk-off run on a wild pitch. The larger the difference between your predicted point spread and the posted point spread, the higher the Margin of Safety.

Playbooks

There are separate Wager to Win Playbooks that supplement *Get In and Win* for each of the major sports: the NFL; college football; the NBA; NCAA basketball; and Major League Baseball. The Playbooks drill deeper into the unique aspects of each sport and provide even more useful information that will deepen your understanding of each game and increase your sports wagering success.

Scorecard

Compounding tables for sports wagering used to show the potential winnings that can be accumulated based on Beginning Capital amounts and estimated Win Rates.

Score Sheets

Used to perform a step-by-step analysis to forecast the total points that each team will score in a game. After forecasting points scored by each team, a predicted point spread can be easily calculated. The Score Sheet is a "bottom-up" analysis of the relevant game factors influencing the actual performance of each specific team.

Value Ratings

A relative measure of a team's overall strength as compared to other teams, expressed in terms of a single number (for example, 108). Value Ratings can be used to forecast a point spread by simply taking the difference between two teams' Value Ratings (adjusted for home field advantage). Carefully assigned and properly maintained, a team's Value Rating can be a comprehensive and accurate measure of the team's most likely performance. Value Ratings provide a "top-down" view of team performance. There are predetermined Value Rating scales for each sport.

Win Rate

The percentage of successful wagers that a sports bettor makes. For example, winning six out of 10 bets results in a 60 percent Win Rate.

Made in the USA
San Bernardino, CA
02 September 2013